TORAH PORTIONS FOR CHILDREN
Shemot
BOOK 2: EXODUS

אֶהְיֶה אֲשֶׁר אֶהְיֶה

I AM WHO I AM

NATALEE HENRY & YEVGENIYA CALENDRILLO

TORAH PORTIONS FOR CHILDREN

Shemot

BOOK 2: EXODUS

Natalee Henry & Yevgeniya Calendrillo

Copyright © Natalee Henry & Yevgeniya Calendrillo, 2023.

Printed in the United States 2023

All rights reserved. This book may not be copied or reprinted for commercial gain or profit. No portion of this book may be reproduced, stored in a retrieval system, transmitted in any form or by any means electronic, mechanical photocopy, recording, or any other except brief quotations in printed reviews, without the prior permission of the Authors and the Publisher. Rights for publishing this book in other languages are to be in written permission by Natalee Henry and Yevgeniya Calendrillo.

Unless otherwise stated, scripture References are from the New American Standard Bible (NASB), and the Tree of Life Version.

This book is a part of the Torah for Children Curriculum. www.torah4children.net

ISBN: 978-1-66640-576-7

Acknowledgments

Thanks to Ken & Lisa Albin, and our Family and Tribe at Save The Nations for your continued love, support, and encouragement throughout our writing journey.

Special thanks to Kiwi Gomes for editing and proofreading, and all the teachers at Save The Nations who have been serving in the children's ministry teaching this curriculum.

Torah Portion Titles

1. Shemot - Names   Page 1
2. Va'era - I Appeared   Page 17
3. Bo - Go   Page 32
4. Beshalach - When He sent   Page 48
5. Yitro - Jethro   Page 64
6. Mishpatim - Rulings   Page 77
7. Terumah - Contributions   Page 95
8. Tetzaveh - You Are To Command   Page 111
9. Ki Tisa - When You Take   Page 126
10. Vayakhel - And Assembled*   Page 141
11. Pekudei - Accounts of*   Page 141

About the Authors   Page 158

About the Book   Page 160

* indicates that these two Torah Portions are read separately during a leap year but are combined during a regular calendar year.

NOTE TO TEACHERS/PARENTS:

Dear Teachers and Parents,

Thank you for choosing to help us equip our children in the Torah Way of the Messiah. We are grateful for you and your time of service.

Each lesson is designed as a guide for teaching the Torah Portions. We encourage you to review the lesson in advance to become familiar with the material provided and allow the Holy Spirit to give you insights for teaching the lesson.

Each lesson is structured so our children will learn from the Torah Portions, and see the connection with Yeshua (Jesus), and the work of the Holy Spirit. Our aim is not just to give information but to teach Torah principles and demonstrate how to use them in their lives.

Every lesson has a general summary of the Torah Portion for the teachers and a lesson summary for the main lesson you will teach for the Torah Portion. With each lesson, there are practical applications and questions. The questions are given at the end of the lesson, however, the teacher can incorporate the questions at any time during the lesson. The practical applications are a great way for the children to connect Torah with their everyday lives.

We have incorporated learning Hebrew with the lesson in video format. Please see the class schedule.

Thanks again for your time and service in helping to equip our children in the Torah Way of the Messiah.

SUGGESTED CLASS SCHEDULE

Welcome

Practical Application Follow-up from the last Lesson in Book 1 *(See the Practical Application Page)*

Torah Portion Lesson

Bathroom Break

Crafts

Snacks

LESSON CONTENTS

Torah Portion Name and Meaning

Torah Portion Theme

Torah Portion Outline

Lesson

    Title & Meaning

    Scriptures

    Theme

    Summary

    Lesson Discussion

    Turning Point *(THIS SECTION IS FOR CHILDREN 9 AND OLDER)*

Practical Applications

Questions and Answer Sheet

Crafts and Instructions

Shemot

"Names"

Torah Portion 13: Shemot

The Hebrew word for this Torah portion is Shemot which means "**Names**"; it is from the first verse of our Torah reading in Exodus chapter 1.

Exodus 1:1 – Now these are the names of *Bnei-Yisrael* who came into Egypt with Jacob, each man with his family:

Scripture Readings:
Exodus 1:1-6, Isaiah 27:6-28, 29:22-23, Matthew 2:1-12, Psalm 99

The Theme of the Torah Portion:
God Hears, God Sees!

Scripture for Theme:

Exodus 2:23-25
Now it came about in *the course of* those many days that the king of Egypt died. And the sons of Israel sighed because of the bondage, and they cried out; and their cry for help because of *their* bondage rose up to God. **24** So God heard their groaning; and God remembered His covenant with Abraham, Isaac, and Jacob. **25** God saw the sons of Israel, and God took notice *of them.*

Torah Portion Outline

- Slavery in Egypt, **Exodus 1:1-22**
- Moses is Born, **Exodus 2:1-10**
- Moses Flees Egypt to Midian, **Exodus 2:11-15**
- Moses Marries Zipporah, **Exodus 2:16-22**
- God Hears, God Sees, **Exodus 2:23-25**
- God Speaks From the Burning Bush, **Exodus 3:1-21**
- Moses Turn to See the Bush, **Exodus 3:1-9**
- God Sends Moses to Pharaoh, **Exodus 3:10-21**
- They Will Not Believe Me, **Exodus 4:1-9**
- I Can't Speak Well, **Exodus 4:10-13**
- Aaron, Moses Mouthpiece, **Exodus 4:14-17**
- Moses Return to Egypt, **Exodus 4:18-31**
- Let My People Go!, **Exodus 5:1-3**
- Bricks without Straw, **Exodus 5:4-20**
- You Made Us a Stench, **Exodus 5:21-23**

LESSON SUMMARY

Things have taken a turn since Joseph died in Egypt for the sons of Jacob. In last week's Torah portion, Jacob adopted Joseph's sons and blessed them, he blessed his twelve sons before he died. Joseph, his brothers, and the officers in Egypt took his body to Hebron to bury him because of the oath he made Joseph swear before his death. At the end of the Torah portion Joseph also died. Joseph told his brothers to remember to take his bones with them when God takes them out of Egypt.

The twelve sons of Jacob are now called the children of Israel or the Hebrew children. They grew and multiplied in the land of Egypt and became a mighty people in Egypt. By this time there was a new ruling Pharaoh who knew nothing about Joseph and how God used him to save the people. Because the children of Israel became so numerous he was afraid that if there was war, they would join with his enemies and help to fight against him. He made them work as slaves and even tried to kill all the boy babies when they were born. The midwives who delivered the babies feared God, they did not listen to Pharaoh nor did they throw them into the Nile River as Pharaoh demanded.

When Moses was born, his parents hid him for three months. They believed he was a special gift from God. When they could no longer hide him, his mother made a wicker basket placed him in it, and put him on the river Nile. His sister was watching the basket. When Pharaoh's daughter saw him, she knew he was one of the Hebrew babies. His sister, knowing who he was, convinced Pharaoh's daughter to get a nurse for him, so she went and called her mother. Pharaoh's daughter named the baby Moses. Moses grew up as an Egyptian in Pharaoh's house but he knew he was an Israelite (descendant of Jacob.)

One day, when Moses was a young man, he went out to visit the location where the people were working. He saw an Egyptian beating one of the slaves and Moses became furious with anger. He struck the Egyptian and the Egyptian died. Moses, afraid of what Pharaoh might do, took the man's body and buried it in the sand. The next day Moses went out again to visit. This time he saw two Israelites fighting, so he said to them, "Why are you fighting each other, aren't you brothers?" One of the men said to him, "Who made you judge and rule over us? Are you going to kill us like you did the Egyptians and bury our bodies in the sand?" Moses became afraid because he thought no one had seen him hiding the man's body. He said to himself, surely Pharaoh must know what I have done and will kill me. So he ran away from Egypt.

Moses fled to Midian where he met his wife Zipporah, the daughter of Jethro, the Priest of Midian. Moses became a shepherd. Moses took the flock of his father-in-law out to pasture one day on the west side of the wilderness in Horeb, the Mountain of God. The angel of God appeared to him in a blazing fire from a bush. Moses noticed the bush was burning but it was not being consumed. He said, "I must turn aside now and see this marvelous sight, why the bush is not burned up." When the Lord saw that he turned aside to look, God called to him from the midst of the bush and said, "Moses, Moses!" And he said, "Here I am." Then He said, "Do not come near here; remove your sandals from your feet, for the place on which you are standing is holy ground." He said also, "I am the God of your father, the God of Abraham, the God of Isaac, and the God of Jacob." Then Moses hid his face, for he was afraid to look at God. **(Exodus 3:3-6)**

God also said to Moses I have seen how the taskmasters are treating My people in Egypt and I hear their cry for help. I know all about their sufferings, so I have come down to deliver them and to bring them to a large land flowing with milk and honey. I am sending you to Pharaoh so you will bring My people, the sons of Israel out of Egypt. I will be with you, and when you leave you will worship on this mountain as a sign to you that I am the one who sent you. **13** Then Moses said to God, "Behold, I am going to the sons of Israel, and I will say to them,

'The God of your fathers has sent me to you.' Now they may say to me, 'What is His name?' What shall I say to them?" **14** God said to Moses, "I AM WHO I AM"; and He said, "Thus you shall say to the sons of Israel, 'I AM has sent me to you.'" **(Exodus 3:13-14)**. Moses was told to go to the leaders of Israel and say to them, the Lord, the God of your fathers, the God of Abraham, Isaac, and Jacob, has appeared to me saying I am about to bring you up out of Egypt. They will listen to you. Together with the elders go to the King of Egypt and say to him, The God of the Hebrews has met with us. Let us go on a three-day journey to the wilderness that we may sacrifice to the Lord our God. I know he will not let you go, so I will stretch out My hand and strike Egypt with My miracles after he will let you go.

LESSON DISCUSSION:
God Hears, God sees!

The children of Israel grew and multiplied greatly. They became a powerful group of people in Egypt just as God told Jacob they would. Pharaoh made them slaves because he was afraid of them. They cried out to God to deliver them.

God wanted to deliver His people, but he needed someone whom He could send to speak for Him. God chose to send Moses. As Moses was caring for his father-in-law's flock God spoke to him from a burning bush. Moses was surprised to see that the bush was on fire but it was not burning up. He turned to see how it could be.

God said to Moses, do not come near and take the shoes off your feet because this place is holy ground. Moses did as God told him. God chose Moses as His servant to go to Egypt and deliver the children of Israel. God spoke to Moses saying, "**7** The Lord said, "I have surely seen the affliction of My people who are in Egypt, and have given heed to their cry because of their taskmasters, for I am aware of their sufferings. **8** So I have come down to deliver them from the power of the Egyptians, and to bring them up from that land to a good and spacious land, to a land flowing with milk and honey," (Exodus 3:7-8).

A voice called to him from the fire, Moses, Moses!

What? The bush is burning but not consumed, and then a voice is speaking from it. Woe, wait a minute! What would be your reaction if you were Moses?

When others treat us unkindly, know that God sees and God hears.

We don't have to try and get revenge or do the same. When we pray and ask God to help, He will help us.

Sometimes, it is because they are afraid of you or because they are hurting and don't know how to get help.

Romans 12:18-20
Do all that you can to live in peace with everyone. **19** Dear friends, never take revenge. Leave that to the righteous anger of God. For the Scriptures say, "I will take revenge; I will pay them back," says the Lord. **20** Instead, "If your enemies are hungry, feed them. If they are thirsty, give them something to drink. In doing this, you will heap burning coals of shame on their heads."

TURNING POINT:

Excuses, Excuses!

How many times have your parents told you to do something but you give them all the excuses why you can't do it?

This was Moses' dilemma! God, His heavenly Father chose him for an assignment but he did not think he was the right person for the job. He told God, "The people might not believe that You sent me." God gave him miraculous signs to show the people. God made his rod turn into a snake and back into a rod again. He also made Moses' hand white with Tzarat (Leprosy) to prove to the people that He sent Moses. Moses still tried to make excuses. He even said to God, "I cannot speak well." God asked Moses, "Who made man's mouth? Or who makes a man mute or deaf, seeing or blind? Is it not I, *Adonai*? Now go! I will be with your mouth and teach you what to say."**(Exodus 4:11-12 TLV)**. Moses was still refusing, and replied, "Please, please, send someone else. Then the anger of *Adonai* was kindled against Moses, so He said, "In fact, Aaron the Levite is your brother. I know that he can speak well. Moreover, he is on his way to meet you! When he sees you, he will be glad in his heart. You are to speak to him and put the words in his mouth. I will be with your mouth and with his, and teach you what to do. He will be your spokesman to the people, so that he may act as a mouthpiece for you, and it will be as if you were as God for him. Now then, you must take this staff in your hand to do the signs." **(Exodus 4:114-17 TLV)**.

Your excuses are not good enough reasons not to do what you are asked to do, whether it is your parents or God. God will send someone to help us to do what He is asking us to do. He has given us the Holy Spirit to be our helper. Will you do what He asks of you?

PRACTICAL APPLICATIONS
God Sees, God Hears; No More Excuses!

FOR CHILDREN 4-6 YEARS OLD

God is always listening and seeing what we do.
Remember to do the right thing even when your parents are not with you.

FOR CHILDREN 7-12 YEARS OLD

Do you often feel the need to make excuses when you are asked to do something, or when you don't do what you are asked to do?

This week, practice doing what you are asked to do without making any excuses. Do the right thing even when no one is watching you, knowing God sees and hears everything.

FOLLOW-UP FROM THE LAST TORAH PORTION

Ask who wants to share from last week's practical application

FOR CHILDREN 4-6 YEARS OLD

Ask your parents to pray for you and to write a blessing for you. Keep the blessing as a reminder that you are a gift from God.

FOR CHILDREN 7-12 YEARS OLD

Galatians 5:22-23 – But the Holy Spirit produces this kind of fruit in our lives: love, joy, peace, patience, kindness, goodness, faithfulness, **23** gentleness, and self-control. There is no law against these things!

Ask the Holy Spirit to help you to be an example to your friends and family and share His fruits with them through you.

QUESTIONS - TEACHERS ANSWER KEY

1. **What is another name for the children of Israel?**
   Hebrews

2. **What is the name God gave Moses to tell the people who He is?**
   I AM WHO I AM

3. **Whom did God send to go with Moses to Egypt?**
   Aaron

4. **Who gave Moses his name?**
   Pharaoh's daughter

5. **How old was Moses when his mother put him in the basket on the river?**
   3 months

6. **What did Pharaoh tell the midwives to do with the baby boys when they were born?**
   He told them to throw the babies in the Nile River

7. **Why did Moses flee Egypt?**
   He was running from Pharaoh because he killed an Egyptian

8. **What is the name of Moses' wife?**
   Zipporah

9. **On what mountain did Moses see the burning bush?**
   Horeb, The Mountain of God

10. **Where did Moses live after he fled Egypt?**
    Midian

QUESTIONS - CHILDREN'S COPY

1. What is another name for the children of Israel?

2. What is the name God gave Moses to tell the people who He is?

3. Whom did God send to go with Moses to Egypt?

4. Who gave Moses his name?

5. How old was Moses when his mother put him in the basket on the river?

6. What did Pharaoh tell the midwives to do with the baby boys when they were born?

7. Why did Moses flee Egypt?

8. What is the name of Moses' wife?

9. On what mountain did Moses see the burning bush?

10. Where did Moses live after he fled Egypt?

CRAFTS SUPPLIES FOR TORAH PORTION SHEMOT

SUPPLIES:
1. 12X12 Black Cardstock Paper
2. Brown Construction Paper
3. Orange Construction Paper
4. Yellow Construction Paper
5. Print Paper
6. Glue Sticks
7. Light Color Pencils
8. Scissors
9. Gems

CRAFTS: THE BURNING BUSH

1. Each child receives black cardstock.
2. They will glue pre-cut bush trunks at the bottom center.
3. They will then receive 5 orange flames each and glue them as shown.

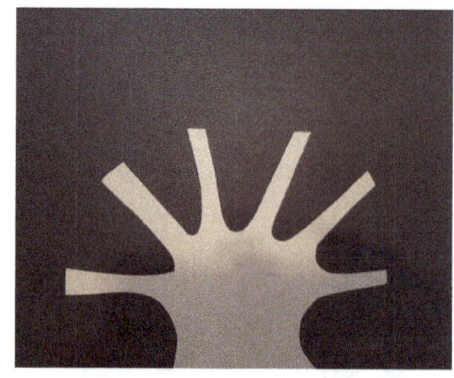

4. Then they will each receive 8 orange flames and glue them on top of the yellow, as shown. They should match.

5. Then each child will receive 8 Scripture verses from Exodus 3 that describe what HaShem said about Himself.
6. They will glue stick those verses, one on each flame.

7. Then they will write at the top in light colored pencil "I AM WHO I AM." and decorate it with gems.
8. At the bottom, they will write "Holy Ground, Holy, Holy."

FINAL WORK

Va'era
"I Appeared"

Torah Portion 14: Va'era

Va'era is the Hebrew word for **"I Appeared"** which is found in the second verse of our Torah portion.

Exodus 6:3 TLV
I appeared to Abraham, to Isaac and to Jacob, as *El Shaddai*. Yet by My Name, *Adonai*, did I not make Myself known to them.

Scripture Readings:
Exodus 6:2-9:35, Ezekiel 28:25-29:21,
Luke 11:14-22, Psalm 46

The Theme of the Torah Portion:

My Name and My Power!

Exodus 9:15-17

Surely by now I could have stretched out My hand and struck you and your people with a plague that would have wiped you off the earth. 16 However, I have let you stand for this reason: to show you My power, and that My Name might be proclaimed throughout all the earth. 17 Yet still you exalt yourself over My people, by not letting them go.

Torah Portion Outline

- Moses Speaks to the Elders of Israel, **Exodus 6:2-15**
- The Names of All the Elders, **Exodus 6:16-30**
- God gave Moses & Aaron a Message for Pharaoh, **Exodus 7:1-13**
- Aaron's Rods Turned into a Snake, **Exodus 7:14-19**
- First Plague - Waters Turned to Blood, **Exodus 7:20-26**
- Second Plague - The Frogs, **Exodus 8:1-11**
- Third Plague - Gnats, **Exodus 8:12-14**
- God Separates the Hebrews from Egyptians, **Exodus 8:15-19**
- Fourth Plague - Flies, **Exodus 8:20-28**
- Fifth Plague - The Animals Die, **Exodus 9:1-7**
- Sixth Plague - Boils, **Exodus 9:8-12**
- Seventh Plague - Hail, **Exodus 9:13-35**

LESSON SUMMARY

Moses returned to Egypt with his brother Aaron. God appeared to Moses and said, "I appeared to Abraham, to Isaac, and to Jacob as El-Shaddai—'God Almighty'—but I did not reveal my name, Yahweh, to them. And I reaffirmed my covenant with them. Under its terms, I promised to give them the land of Canaan, where they were living as foreigners. **(Exodus 6:3-4 NLT)**.

God told Moses that Pharaoh was stubborn and he would refuse to let the people go. Moses went to Pharaoh while he was in the Nile River and said to him, God the God of the Hebrews sent me to you to say; Let My people go, so they can worship Me in the desert. Moses was eighty (80) years old when he went to speak to Pharaoh and Aaron was eighty-three (83) years old. Pharaoh said to Moses and Aaron to prove themselves so I know God sent you. God had told Moses and Aaron that when Pharaoh asked for proof, Aaron should throw down his rod and it would become a serpent (snake), so Aaron threw down his rod. Pharaoh was not afraid, he called his magicians and sorcerers of Egypt. They too threw down their rods, and they became serpents, but the serpent from Aaron's rod swallowed their serpents. Aaron took the serpent by its tail and it became a rod again. This was the first of many signs that God did through Moses and Aaron before Pharaoh let the people go.

Even then Pharaoh refused to let the people go. God sent ten plagues to teach Pharaoh, the king of Egypt, and the Egyptians, that He is the One true God. In this Torah portion, we learn of the first seven plagues that God sent to punish Egypt. He turned the waters into blood, He sent frogs, gnats, and armies of flies. God caused the animals to die, He put boils (sores) upon all the people and animals, and let hail fall like rain.

The first three plagues God caused all of Egypt and the children of Israel to experience. He caused all the waters in Egypt to turn to blood, and he sent frogs that were everywhere, even in the beds and pots and pans that they used for cooking. Pharaoh still refused to let the people go to worship God. He called his magicians who also caused the waters to turn to blood and made frogs appear by sorcery.

The third plague God sent was different. He sent gnats, tiny flies like lice, all over the Land; when Pharaoh called his magicians, they could not cause the gnats to appear. They told Pharaoh we cannot do that, this is a miracle from the finger of God. Pharaoh's magicians knew that God was working but he still refused to let the people go. Every time God sent a plague Pharaoh would ask Moses to pray to God for the plagues to stop, and said he would let the people go, but once the plagues stopped he would change his mind.

After the third plague, God made a separation between His people, the Hebrews (children of Israel), and the Egyptians. Only the Egyptians experienced the remaining seven plagues that God would use to punish Pharaoh and the Egyptians. While in Goshen, God protected His people from the armies of flies He sent, their animals did not die, and neither was there anyone among them with boils, and no hail fell in Goshen. The hail struck down everything that was in the fields, both men and animals, all throughout the land of Egypt. It also struck every plant in the field and broke down every tree. Pharaoh sent, called for Moses and Aaron, and said to them, "I have sinned this time. *Adonai* is righteous, while I and my people are wicked. Pray to *Adonai*— there has been enough of God's thunders and hail! I will let you go. You don't have to stay any longer." Moses said to him, "As soon as I am gone out of the city, I will stretch out my hands to *Adonai*. The thunder will cease and there will be no more hail—so you may know that the earth is *Adonai*'s. But as for you and your servants, I know that you do not yet fear *Adonai Elohim"* **(Exodus 9:25-30)**.

LESSON DISCUSSION: THE POWER AND NAME OF GOD

There are many lessons we can learn from this Torah Portion about God, His power, and His love for the Hebrew people. One of the greatest lessons we can learn is that, God is all-powerful and there is no one like Him. Pharaoh's magicians and sorcerers demonstrated their own power given to them by the many false gods of Egypt, but it was still no match for the God of Abraham, Isaac, and Jacob, Creator of Heaven and Earth.

Exodus 9:13-14

Then *Adonai* said to Moses, "Rise up early in the morning, stand before Pharaoh and say to him: This is what *Adonai* the God of the Hebrews says: 'Let My people go, so they may serve Me. **14** For this time I will send all My plagues to your heart, and on your servants and your people, so that you may know that there is none like Me in all the earth.

God sent Moses numerous times to warn Pharaoh and tell him to let the people go but he refused each time. Even in his stubbornness, God showed him mercy. He gave Pharaoh opportunities to repent and do the right thing.

Exodus 9:15-17

Surely by now I could have stretched out My hand and struck you and your people with a plague that would have wiped you off the earth. **16** However, I have let you stand for this reason: to show you My power, and that My Name might be proclaimed throughout all the earth. **17** Yet still you exalt yourself over My people, by not letting them go.

God is powerful, but He also wants to show us His love. If we choose to do wrong and ignore what He is saying to us, then we will experience the consequences of our actions. God sent His Son, Yeshua, to die for us, while we were still sinners, unworthy of His love.

Why? He wants us to know Him, and through us, declare His name to the whole earth.

Romans 5:8 ESV
But God shows his love for us in that while we were still sinners, Christ died for us.

As children, there are many times your parents, teachers, and other adults will give you instructions but your heart will not want to follow and obey. Like, Pharaoh, you will be tempted to say no and pretend as if you are in control. Remember, no matter how smart you are, you are never in control. God uses your parents and those responsible for you to show you the right way to live, and the things that are acceptable to God.

Will you choose to obey their voice or will you like Pharaoh say no and experience punishment?

TURNING POINT:

THE FINGER OF GOD!

Would you recognize your father's finger if you only saw a picture of his hand?

As children, we sometimes love to copy what our parents do, especially if they are doing something we think is very cool. For example, you might see your dad pick up a basketball with one hand and you might try to copy him; however, you may find your hand is not big enough to hold the ball. You discover that Your hand is not as powerful as your dad's.

Exodus 8:12-15
So Adonai said to Moses, "Tell Aaron, 'Stretch out your staff and strike the dust of the earth, and it will become gnats throughout all the land of Egypt.'" **13** So they did. When Aaron stretched out his hand with his staff and struck the dust of the earth, there were gnats on men and animals. All the dust of the earth became gnats throughout all the land of Egypt. **14** When the magicians attempted the same with their secret arts to bring forth gnats, they could not. There were gnats on men and animals. **15** So the magicians said to Pharaoh, "This is the finger of God." But Pharaoh's heart was hardened, and he did not listen to them—just as Adonai had said.

God did not show Himself to Moses or the Egyptians but the magicians said to Pharaoh, "This is the finger of God."

What did they mean? God had been demonstrating His power to Pharaoh and the Egyptians with the plagues. Pharaoh, however, would call his magicians to demonstrate their power and copy the plagues. This way, Pharaoh was showing Moses and the people that he had his own gods who could do miracles, but the magicians could not copy the third plague. They could not cause gnats to swarm the land. Their hands (power) were not as powerful as God's.

God is all-powerful, and only when we obey him and do what He tells us, can we demonstrate His power the way Moses and Aaron did. When you obey, others will see the FINGER OF GOD!

PRACTICAL APPLICATIONS

BE AWARE OF YOUR ACTIONS!

FOR CHILDREN 4-6 YEARS OLD

Are you being bold like Moses to do the right thing and what God requires?

Are you being like Pharaoh, who does not listen to God?

FOR CHILDREN 7-12 YEARS OLD
When your parents or teachers give you instruction;

Are you being bold like Moses to do the right thing and what God requires? Are you being like Pharaoh, who does not listen to God?

How does being aware of your actions help you when making choices?

FOLLOW-UP FROM THE LAST TORAH PORTION
Ask who wants to share from last week's practical application.

FOR CHILDREN 4-6 YEARS OLD
God is always listening and seeing what we do.
Remember to do the right thing even when your parents are not with you.

FOR CHILDREN 7-12 YEARS OLD
Do you often feel the need to make excuses when you are asked to do something, or when you don't do what you are asked to do?

This week, practice doing what you are asked without making any excuses. Do the right thing even when no one is watching you, knowing God sees and hears everything.

QUESTIONS - TEACHERS ANSWER KEY

1. By what name did God reveal Himself to Abraham?
El Shaddai - God Almighty

2. How old were Moses and Aaron when they spoke to Pharaoh?
Moses 80 and Aaron 83

3. Where was Pharaoh when Moses first spoke to him?
In River Nile

4. What was the first miracle Pharaoh saw?
Aaron's rod turned into a serpent (snake)

5. How many plagues did God send against Egypt?
Ten (10)

6. What did the magicians say about the plague of the gnats?
This is the finger of God

7. What was the message Moses gave to Pharaoh?
God of the Hebrews said; Let My people go so they can worship Me in the desert.

8. How many days did Moses say it was to go and make a sacrifice in the desert?
Three (3) days

9. Where did God say He was also sending the plagues?
To the heart of the people

10. Why didn't God send a plague to wipe out the Egyptians from the earth?
He wanted to show them His power so that His name would be proclaimed all over the earth.

QUESTIONS - CHILDREN'S COPY

1. By what name did God reveal Himself to Abraham?

2. How old were Moses and Aaron when they spoke to Pharaoh?

3. Where was Pharaoh when Moses first spoke to him?

4. What was the first miracle Pharaoh saw?

5. How many plagues did God send against Egypt?

6. What did the magicians say about the plague of the gnats?

7. What was the message Moses gave to Pharaoh?

8. How many days did Moses say it was to go and make a sacrifice in the desert?

9. Where did God say He was also sending the plagues?

10. Why didn't God send a plague to wipe out the Egyptians from the earth?

CRAFTS SUPPLIES FOR TORAH PORTION VA'ERA

SUPPLIES:
1. White Cardstock
2. Markers/Pencils/Crayons
3. Popsicle Sticks
4. Cotton Balls
5. Large Doll Eyes
6. Scissors
7. Glue or Double-Sided Tape
8. Glue Sticks
9. Star Stickers
    All supplies are taken care of*

CRAFTS: FIRST 5 PLAGUES

This week we are going to do the craft for the first 5 plagues of Egypt. Please instruct the students to KEEP these, because we will request that they bring them for Passover Seder.

1. River turning into blood: Distribute pre-cut and pre-drawn cardstocks. Have the kids color it in. Glue the cotton balls to represent the clouds. Glue or stick the popsicle stick with the double-sided scotch tape. Mark which plague this is in the back.

2. Frogs: Distribute pre-cut and pre-drawn card stocks. Have the kids color it in. Glue the doll's eyes on the frog. Glue or stick the popsicle stick with the double-sided scotch tape. Mark which plague this is in the back.

3. Lice: Distribute pre-cut and pre-drawn card stocks. Have the kids color it in. Glue the doll's eyes on the lice. Glue or stick the popsicle stick with the double-sided scotch tape. Mark which plague this is in the back.

4. Mosquitoes: Distribute pre-cut and pre-drawn cardstock. Have the kids color it in. Glue the

doll's eyes on the mosquito. Distribute the other 2 mosquitoes per child. With the glue stick, glue it as shown. Glue or stick the popsicle stick with the double-sided scotch tape. Mark which plague this is in the back.

5. Pestilence on the livestock: Distribute pre-cut and pre-drawn cardstocks. Make the kids color it in. Stick star stickers where shown. Glue or stick the popsicle stick with the double-sided scotch tape. Mark which plague this is in the back.

BO
"GO"

Torah Portion 15: BO

The Hebrew word name of this Torah portion is BO which means **"GO."** It is found in the first verse of our Torah reading for this week.

Exodus 10:1 TLV

Then *Adonai* said to Moses, "**Go** to Pharaoh, because I have hardened his heart and the heart of his servants, so that I might show these My signs in their midst,

Scripture Readings:

Exodus 10:1-13:16, Jeremiah 46:13-28, John 19:31-37, Psalm 77

The Theme of the Torah Portion:

Humble Yourself

Exodus 10:3

So Moses and Aaron went to Pharaoh and said to him, "This is what *Adonai*, the God of the Hebrews, says: How long would you refuse to humble yourself before Me? Let My people go, so they may serve Me.

Torah Portion Outline

- Plague of Locust, **Exodus 10:1-18**
- Plague of Darkness, **Exodus 10:19-24**
- Warning of The Final Plague of Death, **Exodus 11:1- 9**
- A New Beginning for Israel, **Exodus 12:1-11**
- Blood on the Doorposts, **Exodus 12:12-13**
- Feast of Unleavened Bread, **Exodus 12:14-20**
- Preparing the Lamb, **Exodus 12:21-28**
- The Death of the Firstborn and the Children of Israel leaves Egypt, **Exodus 12:29-50**
- Redeeming of the Firstborn in Israel, **Exodus 13:1-16**

LESSON SUMMARY

One would think by this time after experiencing seven devastating plagues, Pharaoh would have humbled himself before God and let the children of Israel go free. Yet, he continually refuses to obey God's voice. God had been showing Pharaoh mercy, but in this Torah portion, God will again demonstrate to Pharaoh, all of Egypt, and the children of Israel that He is the I AM!

Then *Adonai* said to Moses, "Go to Pharaoh, because I have hardened his heart and the heart of his servants, so that I might show these My signs in their midst, **2** and so you may tell your son and your grandchildren what I have done in Egypt, as well as My signs that I did among them, so you may know that I am *Adonai*." **Exodus 10:1-2 TLV.**

God warned Pharaoh to let the people go or else He would send locusts to destroy every tree, green plant, and vegetation in the field that the hail left behind. Pharaoh once again refused to humble himself and obey. The Lord caused an east wind to bring locusts that covered the land. The locusts were plentiful. No one could see the ground. Locusts were everywhere. In Pharaoh's house and his servants' houses. Only in Goshen, where the children of Israel lived, were there no locusts. No one in Egypt had ever seen so many locusts before and have not since that day.

Pharaoh's servants were becoming fearful of Adonai, they said to him, "How long will this man be a snare to us? Send the men, so they may serve *Adonai* their God. Don't you realize yet that Egypt is being destroyed?" Exodus 10:7. Pharaoh did not let the people go because the Lord hardened his heart. God sent darkness upon the land for three days. The darkness covered the land like a thick blanket and all the people could feel it, but there was still light in Goshen. Pharaoh called Moses and said to him that he could take his men and cattle and go worship his God, however, the women and children must stay.

Moses said not so, everyone must go. Pharaoh became angry at Moses. He told Moses to go away from him, that he would never see his face again, and that the next time he saw his face he would die. Moses answered, "You are right, I will never see your face again."

God gave Israel a new beginning, in the month of Aviv (Abib). After that, Adonai gave Moses instructions for the children of Israel before the plague of death. God told Moses to tell the children of Israel to take a lamb or a young goat and prepare a meal to eat. The animal must be without any defect and it must be a year old. They were to choose the animal on the tenth day of the month and on the fourteenth day to kill it and eat at twilight (midnight). They were to roast the entire animal and eat it. He also told them to take a branch of hyssop and use it to smear the blood of the animal on the two doorposts and also over the top of the door. The blood was to mark their houses so that when he, the Angel of Death, passed through Egypt to kill all the firstborns, they would be saved. After this, Pharaoh will let My people go. The children of Israel did all that Moses commanded them to do according to God's word. There were many Egyptians who had seen the plagues and feared God also did as God commanded. Even though the scripture does not directly say that we can infer it because we are told in Exodus 12:38 that there was a mixed multitude in the Exodus out of Egypt. That night a great cry was heard throughout all the land of Egypt as the firstborn died. Pharaoh then called Moses and told him to take his people; the men, women, and children, and their cattle and get out of Egypt now!

LESSON DISCUSSION

One More Plague! – One More Chance!

Now *Adonai* had said to Moses, "I will bring one more plague upon Pharaoh and on Egypt. After that, he will let you go from here. When he lets you go, he will surely thrust you out altogether from here. **2** Speak now into the ears of the people, and let every man ask from his neighbor and every woman from her neighbor for articles of silver and gold." **3** *Adonai* gave the people favor in the eyes of the Egyptians. Indeed, the man Moses was very great in the land of Egypt, in the eyes of Pharaoh's servants and in the eyes of the people. **Exodus 11:1-3**

God gave Pharaoh many chances to humble himself and repent, but he refused. The final plague hurt the heart of Pharaoh. He lost his firstborn son. The one who would one day reign as king in Egypt. The son who should continue his legacy in Egypt. Losing his son was very painful. There was nothing more for Pharaoh to lose. This time he realized that he could no longer refuse to obey.

ONE, TWO, THREE … and COUNTING

Not one, not two, not three, but ten plagues before Pharaoh surrendered. Do you think if Pharaoh had listened to God and asked for forgiveness God would have forgiven him?

How many times do your parents have to talk to you before you obey their voice and do what they tell you to do?

Sometimes when you are enjoying playing a game, watching your favorite show, or talking with your friend it is hard to stop what you are doing to listen to your parents. Doing so is not pleasing to them, but just as God showed Pharaoh mercy, they too are merciful by not punishing you after the first, second, third, or however many chances you get before they begin to lose their patience.

Every day God gives us a chance to do the right things in life. He gave up His firstborn Son, Yeshua, to bring us life.

Colossians 1:15

The Son (Yeshua) is the image of the invisible God, the firstborn over all creation.

When we obey our parents we also are obedient to God.

Yeshua desires to share a meal with us just as the children of Israel ate the lamb together before God walked through Egypt to set them free.

Revelation 3:20

"Look! I stand at the door and knock. If you hear my voice and open the door, I will come in, and we will share a meal together as friends.

TURNING POINT:

A NEW BEGINNING

The children of Israel cried out for freedom, but before God brought them out of Egypt He declared a new beginning for them. He also gave them instructions for what we now know as Passover, the eating of the lamb as a memorial for what He had done as He passed over the doors with the blood in Egypt when all the firstborn died.

Exodus 12: 1-3

Now *Adonai* spoke to Moses and Aaron in the land of Egypt saying, **2** "This month will mark the beginning of months for you; it is to be the first month of the year for you. **3** Tell all the congregation of Israel that on the tenth day of this month, each man is to take a lamb for his family one lamb for the household.

God was not just interested in bringing the children out of Egypt and leaving them to live like the Egyptians. He was taking them into the land He promised their fathers Abraham, Isaac, and Jacob. He wanted them to know they were His people who were to live according to His times and ways. Each year Passover is a reminder for them, and to us, that God is the I AM! He is the one who gives us freedom through Yeshua our Messiah.

Sometimes you might feel as if you want a new beginning. You may want to hang out with new friends or go to a new school.

Have you thought about what it would take for you to have a new beginning? Maybe you will have to change where you live now. You may even need to change how you treat the friends you have right now. Are you kind to your friends or do you treat them harshly like how Pharaoh treated the children of Israel?

God will give you a new beginning when the time is right, in the meantime, allow the Holy Spirit to teach you how to live in obedience to your parents and how to always treat your friends and family kindly.

PRACTICAL APPLICATIONS

FOR CHILDREN 4-6 YEARS OLD

When your parents talk to you, practice doing what they say right away, and don't let them have to tell you twice.

FOR CHILDREN 7-12 YEARS OLD

Is there someone at school or a family member you have been unkind to? Pray to the Father for forgiveness and then ask the Holy Spirit to give you the boldness to apologize to the person.

FOLLOW-UP FROM THE LAST TORAH PORTION

Ask who wants to share from last week's practical application.

FOR CHILDREN 4-6 YEARS OLD

Are you being bold like Moses to do the right thing and what God requires?

Are you being like Pharaoh, who does not listen to God?

FOR CHILDREN 7-12 YEARS OLD

When your parents or teachers give you an instruction;

Are you being bold like Moses to do the right thing and what God requires? Are you being like Pharaoh, who does not listen to God?

How does being aware of your actions help you when making choices?

QUESTIONS - TEACHERS ANSWER KEY

1. What are the final three plagues God sent?
Locusts, darkness, death

2. What kind of animal should be chosen?
Lamb or Goat

3. From what direction did the wind bring the locusts?
East wind

4. How many days were there darkness in Egypt?
Three days

5. What were they to do with the blood?
Smear it on the doorpost and over the top

6. What did the men and women ask their neighbors for?
Articles of silver and gold

7. What day of the month was the animal chosen?
On the tenth day

8. What day of the month was it to be eaten?
On the fourteenth day

9. How old was the animal chosen?
One year old

10. Was the animal boiled or roasted to eat?
Roasted

11. In what month was the new beginning declared for Israel?
Aviv (Abib)

QUESTIONS - CHILDREN'S COPY

1. What are the final three plagues God sent?

2. What kind of animal should be chosen?

3. From what direction did the wind bring the locusts?

4. How many days was there darkness in Egypt?

5. What were they to do with the blood?

6. What did the men and women ask their neighbors for?

7. What day of the week was the animal chosen?

8. What day of the week was it to be eaten?

9. How old was the animal chosen?

10. Was the animal boiled or roasted to eat?

11. In what month was the new beginning declared for Israel?

CRAFTS SUPPLIES FOR TORAH PORTION BO

SUPPLIES:
1. White Cardstock
2. Black Cardstock
3. Markers/Pencils/Crayons
4. Popsicle Sticks
5. Paper Clasps
6. Large Doll Eyes
7. Scissors
8. Glue or Double-Sided Tape
9. Glue Sticks

CRAFTS: LAST 5 PLAGUES OF EGYPT

This week we are going to do the craft for the last 5 plagues of Egypt. Please instruct the students to KEEP these, because we will request that they bring them for the Passover Seder.

1. Boils:

    Distribute pre-cut white cardstock. Have kids outline their hands. Have them draw boils by following the original example. They could be creative! Glue or stick the popsicle stick with the double-sided scotch tape. Mark which plague this is in the back. (No more than 5-6 minutes on this one, please, as #3 and #5 take longer).

    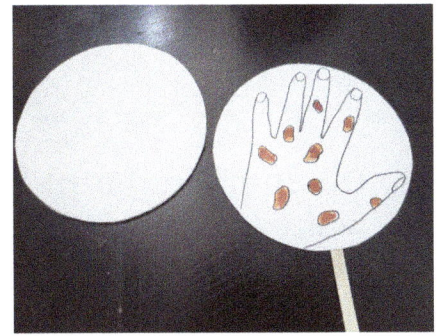

2. Hail: Distribute pre-cut and pre-drawn card stocks. May the kids color it in. Also, distribute pre-cut small white card stock pieces that represent hail (4 per child). The kids could use a glue stick to glue it in random spots. Glue or stick the popsicle stick with the double-sided scotch tape. Mark which plague this is in the back.

3. Locusts: Distribute pre-cut and pre-drawn card stocks. Have the kids color it in. Glue the doll's eyes on the locust. Using paper clasps, attach the leg to the body. (There are holes in the paper already). Glue or stick the popsicle stick with the double-sided scotch tape. Mark which plague this is in the back.

4. Darkness: Distribute pre-cut black cardstock. Have the kids draw a tree and eyes, as shown in the original. Glue or stick the popsicle stick with the double-sided scotch tape. Mark which plague this is in the back. (No more than 5-6 minutes on this one, as #5 takes longer).

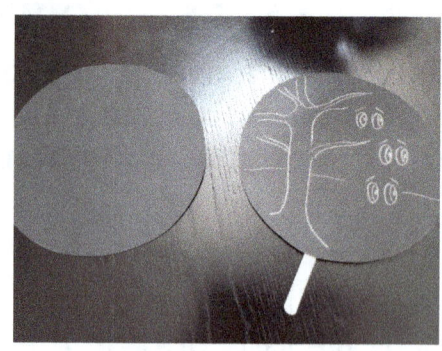

5. Death of firstborn: Distribute pre-cut white cardstock. Using glue, have the kids glue popsicle sticks to represent the door, as shown on the original. Have them draw the door in as shown. Have them mark the doorpost with the red marker or crayon as shown. Glue or stick the popsicle stick with the double-sided scotch tape. Mark which plague this is in the back.

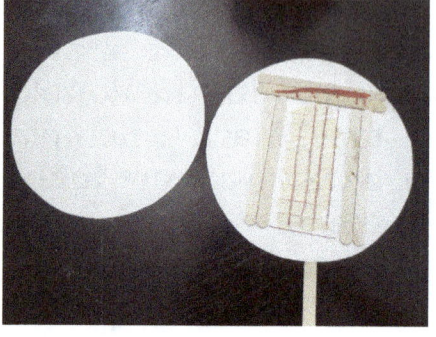

BESHALACH

"When He Sent"

Torah Portion 16: Beshalach

The name of this week's Torah reading is the Hebrew word Beshalach, which means *"when he sent."* It is found in the first verse of our Torah reading.

Exodus 13:17 ArtScroll Tanach
It happened **when Pharaoh sent out** the people that God did not lead them by way of the land of the Philistines, because it was near, for God said, "Perhaps the people will reconsider when they see a war, and they will return to Egypt."

Scripture Readings:
Exodus 13:17-17:16, Judges 4:4-5:31, Matthew 14:22-23, Psalm 66

The Theme of the Torah Portion:

God Goes Before Us!

Exodus 13:21-22 TLV

Adonai went before them in a pillar of cloud by day to lead the way and in a pillar of fire by night to give them light. So they could travel both day and night. **22** The pillar of cloud by day and the pillar of fire by night never departed from the people.

Torah Portion Outline

- The Route to the Promised Land, **Exodus 13:17-22**
- Pharaoh Chases After Israel, **Exodus 14:1-4**
- Israel Panics and Grumbles, **Exodus 14:9-12**
- God's Assurance, **Exodus 14:13-18**
- Parting of the Reed (Red) Sea, **Exodus 14:19-30**
- Moses' Song, **Exodus 15:1-19**
- Miriam's Song, **Exodus 15:20-26**
- The Journey in the Wilderness Begins, **Exodus 16:1-3**
- Manna From Heaven, **Exodus 16:4-12**
- Quails Fall Like Rain, **Exodus 16:13-16**
- Equal Portions of Mana, **Exodus 16:17-22**
- Preparing for the Sabbath, **Exodus 16:23-36**
- Water from the Rock, **Exodus 17:1-7**
- The Amalekites Strike, **Exodus 17:8-14**

LESSON SUMMARY

The children of Israel marched out of Egypt like a great army. Moses carried the bones of Joseph with them when they left Egypt. Not wanting the children of Israel to change their minds at the first sight of trouble, God did not lead them through the land of the Philistines, instead, He brought them around the desert opposite the Reed Sea. Not long after the children of Israel left Egypt Pharaoh had a change of heart. Pharaoh gathered six hundred (600) of his best chariots and all the chariots of Egypt in hot pursuit of the Israelites. Pharaoh and his army chased after them, but Adonai caused the wheels of the chariots to fall off. He also put a cloud between them and the children of Israel that caused them to be in darkness while the Israelites had light.

When the children of Israel saw that the Egyptians were coming after them and the Reed (Red) Sea was before them, they felt trapped with nowhere to run. They began to argue with Moses, saying, why did you bring us out here to die? Were there not enough graves in Egypt to bury us? Moses told the people to be still and see God's salvation. Adonai told Moses to stretch his rod over the sea. Moses did as God commanded him and the waters of the sea parted and stood up like columns. The children of Israel crossed to the other side on dry ground. When all the children of Israel crossed the Reed Sea, Pharaoh and his army also were trying to go through the sea, but Adonai commanded Moses to stretch his rod over the sea again and the waters of the sea covered the Egyptians. Pharaoh and all his men died before the eyes of the Israelites. After seeing how God delivered them from the hands of the Egyptians, Moses and the people sang a song of praise and thanksgiving to Adonai.

As they traveled along their journey in the desert the people became thirsty and hungry. In Marah they found water but it was too bitter for them to drink. The people grumbled and complained to Moses and Aaron once more, but God miraculously made the water sweet so they could drink it. When they were hungry God gave them bread (Manna) from heaven in the morning and quail to fall like rain in the evening because of their grumblings. God provided Manna for them each morning. The people were commanded to gather the manna six days of the week but not on the seventh day because it was a day of rest. It is the Sabbath day for Adonai. They were told to take just enough for each day, cook it, and eat it. They were also instructed not to leave any of the manna uneaten until the next day because it would stink. On the sixth day, they should collect a double portion to last for the sixth and seventh days. Those who did as Adonai commanded on the sixth day had enough manna for both days, whether they gathered too little or too much for their families. Some did not obey and went out on the seventh day to gather manna but they found none. Aaron was commanded to take some of the manna and put it in a jar so that it would be a testimony to future generations. This jar was later placed in the Ark of the Covenant.

Further along the journey, the people thirsted again for water but no water was in Rephidim. God commanded Moses to strike a rock with his rod and water came gushing out. The Amalekites attacked the children of Israel but Joshua and the men of Israel defeated them while Moses stood on the mountain with his rod stretched over them.

LESSON DISCUSSION
God Goes Before Us!

God did not want the children to become discouraged and change their minds at the first sight of war so He did not lead them from Egypt through the land of the Philistines. Instead, He took them through the desert. Leaving Egypt, the children of Israel first camped at Succoth in Ethaim. God was before them as a pillar of cloud by day and as a pillar of fire by night to give them light. He was always with the people. While they camped in the wilderness by the sea, Pharaoh had a change of heart and mind. He questioned why he let the children of Israel go from serving him. He took his best chariots and his army with him to pursue the children of Israel because he wanted to force them to return to Egypt. When the children of Israel saw Pharaoh and his army coming they were afraid. They had an army behind them and a sea in front of them with nowhere to go.

What would you have done? Would you have been like the Israelites and complained and grumbled against Moses or would you have remembered all the miracles God did in Egypt to deliver you from Pharaoh and the Egyptians? Exodus 14:11-13

I can't begin to imagine how the children of Israel felt, but I know that sometimes it is hard to remember that God is with us and that He goes before us when we are in a difficult situation.

God did not get angry with the children of Israel. He gave Moses instructions so the people would see that He is still the God who goes before them and protects them from the enemy behind.

Exodus 14:13-16, 19-20 TLV

13 But Moses said to the people, "Don't be afraid! Stand still, and see the salvation of *Adonai*, which He will perform for you today. You have seen the Egyptians today, but you will never see them again, ever! **14** *Adonai* will fight for you, while you hold your peace." **15** Then *Adonai* said to Moses, "Why are you crying to Me? Tell *Bnei-Yisrael* to go forward. **16** Lift up your staff, stretch out your hand over the sea, and divide it. Then *Bnei-Yisrael* will go into the midst of the sea on dry ground. **19** Then the angel of God, who went before the camp of Israel, moved and went behind them. Also the pillar of cloud moved from in front and stood behind them, **20** and so came between the camp of Egypt and the camp of Israel—there was the cloud and the darkness over here, yet it gave light by night over there—neither one came near the other all night long.

God saved the children of Israel that day from the hands of the Egyptians, and He continues to save those who call on His name. Whenever you are in a difficult situation and you don't see any way for things to become better, remember you are not alone. Call on the name of Adonai. He will deliver you just as He delivered the children of Israel.

Psalm 92:15-16 TLV

15 When he calls on Me, I will answer him. I will be with him in trouble, rescue him, and honor him. **16** With long life will I satisfy him and show him My salvation."

Quiet your heart and allow the Holy Spirit (Ruach HaKodesh) to speak.

Exodus 15:2-3 TLV — *Adonai* is my strength and song, and He has become my salvation. This is my God, and I will glorify Him, my father's God, and I will exalt Him. **3** *Adonai* is a warrior—*Adonai* is His Name!

TURNING POINT:

DON'T STONE ME!

Have you ever heard the phrase "Don't stone the messenger?"

It is used when someone is angry at a person who delivers a message that is not pleasing to the person who receives it. Here we see it plays out with Moses and the children of Israel. Moses is God's Messenger, who was sent by God to deliver them from Egypt. Along the way, they find themselves in situations that make them uncomfortable, so they argue and complain against Moses.

Moses and the people were traveling through the wilderness and they camped in Rephidim but there was no water. The people grumbled and argued with Moses.

Exodus 17:1-3 NASB

1 Then all the congregation of the sons of Israel journeyed by stages from the wilderness of Sin, according to the command of the Lord, and camped at Rephidim, and there was no water for the people to drink. **2** Therefore the people quarreled with Moses and said, "Give us water that we may drink." And Moses said to them, "Why do you quarrel with me? Why do you test the Lord?" **3** But the people thirsted there for water; and they grumbled against Moses and said, "Why, now, have you brought us up from Egypt, to kill us and our children and our livestock with thirst?"

Throughout their journey, the people argued and complained over and over against Moses because they were either thirsty or hungry. It was God who brought them through the Sea of Reeds (Red Sea), He made the bitter waters at Marah sweet for them to drink, and He also gave them bread (Manna) from heaven and quail to eat.

There was no denying it was God in charge, so why grumble at Moses?

What could Moses do?

Moses cried out to God, saying, *"What shall I do to this people?* ***A little more and they will stone me."*** Exodus 17:4

God told Moses, "Pass before the people and take with you some of the elders of Israel; and take in your hand your staff with which you struck the Nile, and go. Behold, I will stand before you there on the rock at Horeb; and you shall strike the rock, and water will come out of it, that the people may drink." And Moses did so in the sight of the elders of Israel. He named the place Massah and Meribah because of the quarrel of the sons of Israel, and because they tested the Lord, saying, "Is the Lord among us, or not?" **Exodus 17:5-7**

What can we learn from this story?

- Everyone is a messenger.
- Your parents are messengers assigned by God to care for you.
- Your teachers are messengers assigned by the school to watch over you while you are there.
- Your friends are messengers; choose Godly friends.
- You are a messenger sent by God during this time of life, be ready to listen and obey His voice.

Next time someone gives you a message, "Don't stone the messenger", ask the Lord what to do and help you recognize why you are angry.

Proverbs 15:1 NASB A gentle answer turns away wrath, But a harsh word stirs up anger.

PRACTICAL APPLICATIONS
Choose your words wisely!

FOR CHILDREN 4-6 YEARS OLD
Ask your parents to help you learn Proverbs 15:1 and explain in your own words what it means.

Proverbs 15:1 NASB
A gentle answer turns away wrath, But a harsh word stirs up anger.

FOR CHILDREN 7-12 YEARS OLD
Learn Proverbs 15:1 and explain in your own words what it means.

Proverbs 15:1 NASB
A gentle answer turns away wrath, But a harsh word stirs up anger.

FOLLOW-UP FROM THE LAST TORAH PORTION
Ask who wants to share from last week's practical application.

When your parents talk to you, practice doing what they say right away, and don't let them have to tell you twice.

FOR CHILDREN 7-12 YEARS OLD
Is there someone at school or a family member you have been unkind to? Pray to the Father for forgiveness and then ask the Holy Spirit to give you the boldness to apologize to the person.

QUESTIONS - TEACHERS ANSWER KEY

1. **Whose bones were carried out of Egypt?**
   Joseph

2. **In what way did God go before the children of Israel?**
   Pillar of cloud by day and pillar of fire by night

3. **What is the name of the sea they had to cross?**
   Reed Sea or Red Sea

4. **How many of Pharaoh's best chariots were taken to pursue Israel?**
   600

5. **What did Moses tell the people when they were afraid of the Egyptians?**
   Stand still and see God's Salvation

6. **What is the name of the place God made the bitter water sweet?**
   Marah

7. **Who attacked the children of Israel after they crossed the sea?**
   Amalekites

8. **How many days were the people to collect Manna?**
   Six (6)

9. **On which day were they allowed to collect a double portion of Manna?**
   Sixth (6th)

10. **Why were they not allowed to gather manna on the seventh day?**
    It was the Lord's Sabbath. Or Day of rest

QUESTIONS - CHILDREN'S COPY

1. Whose bones were carried out of Egypt?

2. In what way did God go before the children of Israel?

3. What is the name of the sea they had to cross?

4. How many of Pharaoh's best chariots were taken to pursue Israel?

5. What did Moses tell the people when they were afraid of the Egyptians?

6. What is the name of the place God made the bitter water sweet?

7. Who attacked the children of Israel after they crossed the sea?

8. How many days were the people to gather Manna?

9. On which day were they allowed to collect a double portion of Manna?

10. Why were they not allowed to gather manna on the seventh day?

CRAFTS SUPPLIES FOR TORAH PORTION BESHALACH

SUPPLIES:
1. Beige 12 x 12 Cardstock
2. Blue Construction Paper
3. White Cardstock
4. Glue and Glue Sticks
5. Markers/Pencils/Crayons
6. Scissors
7. Fish and Ocean Life Stickers

CRAFTS: CROSSING THE SEA

1. Each child will get 2 pieces of 8 ½" by 11" blue construction paper.
2. They will roll both papers twice.
3. They will cut on the straight line on one side of each piece of paper, approximately ½" distance from each cut.

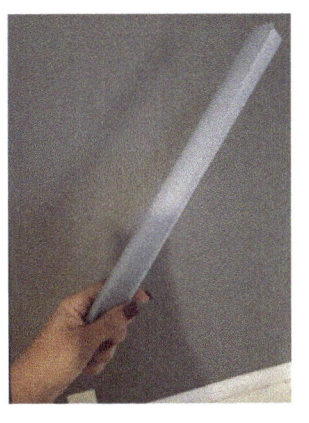
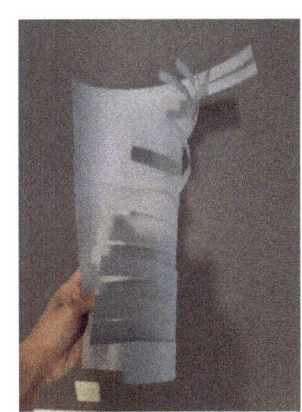

4. Then they will get pre-cut and pre-drawn Moses, Aaron, Miriam, and a donkey. They will color them in.
5. Then they will fold on the fold line as shown.

6. Then they will glue the blue construction paper pieces on top of beige 12x12 cardstock as shown.

7. They will then glue Moses/Aaron/Miriam/donkey in the middle, between the blue papers.

8. Each child will use a few fish and ocean plant stickers in random spots.

FINAL WORK

Yitro

"Jethro"

Torah Portion 17: Yitro

The name of this week's Torah portion is **Yitro**, it is Hebrew for the name of **Jethro**, Moses' father-in-law. It is found in the first verse of our reading.

Exodus 18:1

Now **Jethro**, the priest of Midian and Moses' father-in-law, heard about everything God had done for Moses and for His people Israel, and how Adonai had brought Israel out of Egypt.

Scripture Readings:

Exodus 18:1-20:26, Isaiah 6:1–7:6, 9:5–7, Matthew 19:16–26, Psalm 19

The Theme of the Torah Portion:

God's Chosen People

Exodus 19:5

Now then, if you listen closely to My voice, and keep My covenant, then you will be My own treasure from among all people, for all the earth is Mine.

Torah Portion Outline

- Moses' Father-in-law Jethro Visits Him, **Exodus 18:1-12**

- Jethro's Advice, **Exodus 18:13-27**

- God Speaks to Moses on Mount Sinai, **Exodus 19:1-24**

- The Ten Words (Commandments), **Exodus 20:1-17**

LESSON SUMMARY

This week's Torah portion begins with Moses' father-in-law visiting him in the wilderness of Sinai. He brought with him Moses' wife Zipporah and their two sons. One son was named Gershom because Moses said, "I have been an outsider in a foreign land," and the name of the other son was Eliezer, because he said, "For my father's God is my help, and delivered me from the sword of Pharaoh." Jethro was excited to hear all about how God had delivered them from Egypt. He rejoiced and praised Adonai. He offered a burnt offering and sacrifice declaring Adonai is the one true God. Jethro gave Moses advice on how to judge the people by choosing elders from each tribe who could help share the burden with him. Moses listened to his father-in-law and did everything he told him to do.

In the third month after leaving Egypt God spoke with Moses on top of the Mountain at Sinai. He gave Moses instructions to give to the people. So Moses came down the mountain and gathered all the elders and the people and told them what Adonai said. All the people answered Moses, "All that Adonai said, we will do." Moses reported to Adonai what the people had said. Adonai said to Moses, I will be coming down to you in a thick cloud. Go and sanctify the people so they can draw near to me. Be ready in three days.

"In the morning of the third day, there was thundering and lightning, a thick cloud on the mountain, and the blast of an exceedingly loud shofar. All the people in the camp trembled." Exodus 19:16 TLV. —

God spoke to Moses saying, warn the people not to come up the mountain. Moses, replied You have instructed us to set boundaries so no one could come up. Then He said to Moses go down and bring Aaron with you up the mountain but don't allow anyone else to come, not even the priest, lest God become angry. On the Mountain, Moses received the Ten Words (Commandments).

LESSON DISCUSSION

Today we are taking a look at the Ten Words, or Ten Commandments which God gave to guide us into living a life pleasing to Him.

NOTE TO TEACHERS: After reading each commandment, please have children explain what it means in their own words and discuss how to apply the commandment to their everyday lives.

THE TEN WORDS: EXODUS 20:1-17 TLV

1 Then God spoke all these words saying,

2 (א) "I am *Adonai* your God, who brought you out of the land of Egypt, out of the house of bondage.

3 (ב) "You shall have no other gods before Me. 4 Do not make for yourself a graven image[d], or any likeness of anything that is in heaven above or on the earth below or in the water under the earth. 5 Do not bow down to them, do not let anyone make you serve them. For I, *Adonai* your God, am a jealous God, bringing the iniquity of the fathers upon the children to the third and fourth generations of those who hate Me, 6 but showing lovingkindness to the thousands of generations of those who love Me and keep My *mitzvot*.

7 (ג) "You must not take the Name of *Adonai* your God in vain, for *Adonai* will not hold him guiltless that takes His Name in vain.

8 (ד) "Remember *Yom Shabbat*, to keep it holy. 9 You are to work six days, and do all your work, 10 but the seventh day is a *Shabbat* to *Adonai* your God. In it you shall not do any work—not you, nor your son, your daughter, your male servant, your female servant, your cattle, nor the outsider that is within your gates. 11 For in six days *Adonai* made heaven and earth, the sea, and all that is in them, and rested on the seventh day. Thus *Adonai* blessed *Yom Shabbat*, and made it holy.

12 (ה) "Honor your father and your mother, so that your days may be long upon the land which *Adonai* your God is giving you.

13 (ו) "Do not murder.

14 (ז) "Do not commit adultery.

15 (ח) "Do not steal.

16 (ט) "Do not bear false witness against your neighbor.

17 (י) "Do not covet your neighbor's house, your neighbor's wife, his manservant, his maidservant, his ox, his donkey, or anything that is your neighbor's."

Yeshua was obedient to the Father's commandments. Yeshua told His disciples and the people, that everything He spoke and did is what He learned from the Father. He also said that keeping the commandments is one way we prove to Him, and others, that we love Him.

John 14:15 TLV
"If you love me, you will keep my commands.

TURNING POINT:

Gods of Silver and Gold!

Exodus 20:22-23 TLV
Then *Adonai* said to Moses, "Say this to *Bnei-Yisrael*: You yourselves have seen that I have spoken to you from heaven. **23** Do not make gods of silver alongside Me, and do not make gods of gold for yourselves.

In this Torah portion, God warns the children of Israel not to make any god of silver and gold and worship it, and Him. They only should worship God alone.

God does not want us to make any image of silver or gold to be a god either. He does not want us to have any other god but Him. He wants us to choose Him alone. A god of silver and gold can be represented by many things. Anything you give your attention to more than you give attention to God becomes a god of silver or gold.

Is there anything that you desire and give attention to more than how you spend time with Godly things?

When you spend time reading Torah or being obedient to your parents you are honoring God. If you choose not to obey then your disobedience is like making a god of silver and gold.

PRACTICAL APPLICATIONS
Honoring God!

FOR CHILDREN 4-6 YEARS OLD
When you honor your parents you honor God.
Honor your parents this week in your obedience.

FOR CHILDREN 7-12 YEARS OLD
Each day this coming week, choose two of the Ten Words (Commandments) to learn and apply them as you go through your day.

FOLLOW-UP FROM THE LAST TORAH PORTION
Ask who wants to share from last week's practical application
Choose your words wisely!

FOR CHILDREN 4-6 YEARS OLD
Ask your parents to help you learn Proverbs 15:1 and explain in your own words what it means.

Proverbs 15:1 NASB
A gentle answer turns away wrath, But a harsh word stirs up anger.

FOR CHILDREN 7-12 YEARS OLD
Learn Proverbs 15:1 and explain in your own words what it means.

Proverbs 15:1 NASB
A gentle answer turns away wrath, But a harsh word stirs up anger.

QUESTIONS - TEACHERS ANSWER KEY

1. **What was the name of Moses' father-in-law?**
   Jethro

2. **On which mountain did God give the Ten Words (Commandments)?**
   Mount Sinai

3. **Give the name of Moses' two sons.**
   Gershom and Eliezer

4. **Who was Moses' wife?**
   Zipporah

5. **What are the First and Fourth Commandments?**
   (1st) I am Adonai your God, who brought you out of Egypt, out of the house of bondage.
   (4th) Remember the Sabbath day to keep it holy

6. **What was Jethro's declaration about God?**
   He is the One true God

7. **After how many days did God say He was coming down to talk with the people?**
   Three days

8. **Who was allowed to go up the mountain with Moses?**
   Aaron

9. **What did the people need to do before they could draw near to God?**
   Sanctify themselves

10. **How did God say He was coming down to talk with Moses and the people?**
    In a thick cloud

QUESTIONS - CHILDREN'S COPY

1. What was the name of Moses' father-in-law?

2. On which mountain did God give the Ten Words (Commandments)?

3. Give the name of Moses' two sons.

4. Who was Moses' wife?

5. What are the First and Fourth Commandments?

6. What was Jethro's declaration about God?

7. After how many days did God say He was coming down to talk with the people?

8. Who was allowed to go up the mountain with Moses?

9. What did the people need to do before they could draw near to God?

10. How did God say He was coming down to talk with Moses and the people?

CRAFTS SUPPLIES FOR TORAH PORTION YITRO

SUPPLIES:
1. Black Cardstock 12x12
2. Gold Cardstock 8 ½" by 11"
3. Glue
4. Glue Stick
5. White Cardstock
6. White Print Paper
7. Sequins
8. Gems
9. Stickers

CRAFTS: THE 10 COMMANDMENTS

1. Children will receive 2 black pieces of cardstock glued together like a booklet.
2. They will also receive 2 pieces of gold cardstock to represent the stones. They will glue them on the black cardstock, 1 on each side.

3. They will receive 10 letters to represent the Ten Commandments, from Aleph to Yod (yay for another opportunity to review the letters). They will be asked to glue them to the gold cardstock, in the correct order, 5 on each side.
4. The kids will receive cut-outs of the 10 commandments, verses straight from the Scriptures. They will glue them next to each letter.
5. Then the kids will decorate around it with gems, stones, sequins, and stickers.

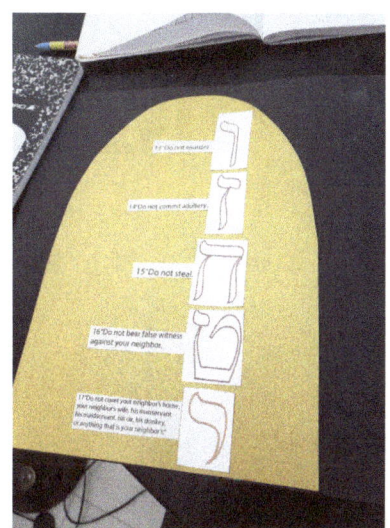

FINAL WORK

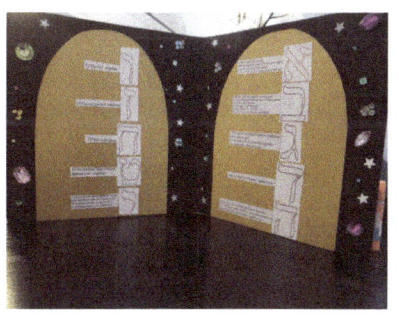

MISHPATIM

"Rulings"

Torah Portion 18: Mishpatim

The name of this Torah Portion is Mishpatim. It is the Hebrew word translated as rulings. It is found in the first verse of our Torah reading.

Exodus 21:1 CJB

These are the ***rulings*** you are to present to them.

Scripture Readings:

Exodus 21:1-24:18, 2 Kings 12:1-17, Matthew 17:22-27, Psalm 72

The Theme of the Torah Portion:

Unity in obedience

Exodus 24:1-3 TLV

Then to Moses He said, "Come up to *Adonai*, you and Aaron, Nadab and Abihu, and the seventy elders of Israel, and worship from afar. **2** Moses alone is to approach *Adonai*, but the others may not draw near, nor are the people to go up with him." **3** So Moses came and told the people all the words of *Adonai* as well as all the ordinances. All the people answered with one voice and said, "All the words which *Adonai* has spoken, we will do." **4** So Moses wrote down all the words of *Adonai*, then rose up early in the morning, and built an altar below the mountain, along with twelve pillars for the twelve tribes of Israel.

Torah Portion Outline

- Rulings Concerning Servants, **Exodus 21:1-11**
- Rulings Concerning Violence, **Exodus 21:12-26**
- Animal Control Rulings, **Exodus 21:27-36**
- Responsibility for Property, **Exodus 22:1-15**
- Moral and Ceremonial Principles, **Exodus 22:16-31**
- Justice for All, **Exodus 23:1-9**
- The Sabbath, **Exodus 23:10-13**
- Three Annual Feasts, **Exodus 23:14-19**
- God's Protection and the Promises, **Exodus 23:20-23**
- Israel Affirms the Covenant, **Exodus 24:1-8**
- On the Mountain of God, **Exodus 24:9-18**

LESSON SUMMARY

In last week's Torah portion, we learned the Ten Words God gave to Moses to teach the children of Israel. In this week's portion, we continue to read about the other rulings or rules (commandments) that God gave them to govern their daily lives. The Torah reading teaches how to treat each other, and how to treat someone who becomes a servant, how to handle violence within the community, and how to handle unruly animals. Each person is responsible for caring for their neighbor and their animals whether they are kind or unfriendly. "Don't abuse or take advantage of strangers; you, remember, were once strangers in Egypt **(Exodus 22:21)**.

The Torah also warns us about gossip and being cruel to strangers, the poor, and animals. "Don't pass on malicious gossip. "Don't link up with a wicked person and give corrupt testimony. Don't go along with the crowd in doing evil and don't mess up your testimony in a case just to please the crowd. And just because someone is poor, don't show favoritism in a dispute. "If you find your enemy's ox or donkey loose, take it back to him. If you see the donkey of someone who hates you lying helpless under its load, don't walk off and leave it. Help it up. "When there is a dispute concerning your poor, don't tamper with the justice due them. "Stay clear of false accusations. Don't contribute to the death of innocent and good people. I don't let the wicked off the hook. "Don't take bribes. Bribes blind perfectly good eyes and twist the speech of good people. "Don't take advantage of a stranger. You know what it's like to be a stranger; you were strangers in Egypt" **(Exodus 23:1-9 Message Bible, MSG).**

We are also reminded to honor the Sabbath and God's feast days, and not to worship any other gods. "Work for six days and rest the seventh so your ox and donkey may rest and your servant and migrant workers may have time to get their needed rest. "Listen carefully to everything I tell you. Don't pay attention to other gods—don't so much as mention their names. "Three times a year you are to hold a festival

for me. "Hold the spring Festival of Unraised (Unleavened) Bread when you eat unraised (Unleavened) bread for seven days at the time set for the month of Abib, as I commanded you. That was the month you came out of Egypt. No one should show up before me empty-handed. "Hold the summer Festival of Harvest when you bring in the firstfruits of all your work in the fields. "Hold the autumn(fall) Festival of Ingathering at the end of the season when you bring in the year's crops. "Three times a year all your males are to appear before the Master, God. "Don't offer the blood of a sacrifice to me with anything that has yeast in it. "Don't leave the fat from my festival offering out overnight. "Bring the choice first produce of the year to the house of your God. "Don't boil a kid in its mother's milk."
(Exodus 23:12-19 MSG)

The Lord reminded the people that He is the One who watches over them. He sent His angel to guard and lead them into the land He promised Abraham. They were to obey Him and were not to become rebellious. He would continue to fight for them, but if they followed and served other gods He would put on them all the diseases He put on the Egyptians. Moses, Aaron, Nadab, Abihu, and seventy of the elders of Israel climbed the mountain to worship God, but only Moses was allowed to go near God. Moses wrote down all the instructions that God gave him on Mount Sinai, the mountain of God. He came down and told the people all that God said, the people responded, "All that God has spoken we will do." Moses got up early the next morning and built an Altar at the foot of the mountain using twelve pillar stones for the twelve tribes of Israel and offered sacrifices and worshiped God. Moses returned to the mountain with Joshua. God gave him tablets of stone with the teachings and commandments that He wrote to instruct the people. Moses spent forty days and forty nights on the mountain with God.

LESSON DISCUSSION

This Torah portion seems like it is filled with a list of things we should do and things we should not do, but it is much more than a list of "dos" and "don'ts." God cares about His people. He cares about our relationship with Him and also our relationship with others. He is concerned with the way we value things. He wants us to understand that we should treat others and their possessions with the same love and respect we do for our own.

What do you think your home would look and sound like if your parents did not have rules for you to follow?
- If they allowed you to do and say whatever you choose?
- If the house did not get cleaned?
- If you were allowed to watch TV and listen to the radio at the same time?
- If they said nothing when you and your brother or sister are fighting?
- What if the dog was allowed to go potty in the house and no one would clean the mess?
- What if your parents went to work every day and did not get paid?

All these what 'ifs' are the reasons why God, our heavenly Father gave us rules to follow. If He allows everyone to do and say whatever we choose without boundaries, He would not be a loving Father.

His rules are not about "dos" and "don'ts" but they are means by which He demonstrates His love toward us and we in return demonstrate our love towards Him by obeying His rulings.

God demonstrated His love for the children of Israel when He delivered them out of Egypt. He demonstrated His love towards us by sending His Son, Yeshua to die for us.

Romans 5:8 Amplified Bible — But God clearly shows *and* proves His own love for us, by the fact that while we were still sinners, Christ died for us.

Yeshua said that we are to show love towards each other because it is a sign that we love Him and the Father.

John 13:33-35 NASB — Little children, I am with you a little while longer. You will seek Me; and as I said to the Jews, now I also say to you, 'Where I am going, you cannot come.' 34 A new commandment I give to you, that you love one another, even as I have loved you, that you also love one another. 35 By this all men will know that you are My disciples, if you have love for one another."

The Holy Spirit helps us to demonstrate our love for Yeshua and our heavenly Father.

Galatians 5:22-23 MSG — But what happens when we live God's way? He brings gifts into our lives, much the same way that fruit appears in an orchard—things like affection for others, exuberance about life, serenity. We develop a willingness to stick with things, a sense of compassion in the heart, and a conviction that a basic holiness permeates things and people. We find ourselves involved in loyal commitments, not needing to force our way in life, able to marshal and direct our energies wisely.

TURNING POINT:

Doing what is right even when it is not popular!

This week's turning point is from the Haftorah portion of our reading in 2 Kings 12:1-17. In our Torah reading we are warned not to follow the crowd and do evil or join in a dispute to pervert justice (Exodus 23:1-3). Years later when Kings began to rule in Israel, some kings did what was right according to the rulings of God in the Torah and some did not do right. Even the people turned their back on God and worshiped idols from other nations.

There was a priest by the name of Jehoiada who along with the people made a covenant before God to restore Torah and order among the people. That year Jehoash (Joash) became king at seven years old. He did what was pleasing to God. He made preparations to repair God's temple. He gave instructions to the priest to collect money for the work to be done. However, the priest neglected to do as the king commanded.

2 Kings 12:6-11 — But it came about that in the twenty-third year of King Jehoash, the priests had not repaired *any* damage to the house. **7** So King Jehoash summoned Jehoiada the priest, and the *other* priests, and said to them, "Why do you not repair damage to the house? Now then, you are not to take *any more* money from your acquaintances, but give it up for the damage to the house." **8** The priests then agreed that they would not take *any more* money from the people, nor would they repair damage to the house. **9** Instead, Jehoiada the priest took a chest and drilled a hole in its lid and put it beside the altar, on the right side as one comes into the house of the Lord; and the priests who guarded the threshold put in it all the money that was brought into the house of the Lord. **10** When they saw that there was a great *amount of* money in the chest, the king's scribe and the high priest went up and tied *it* up in bags, and counted the money that was found in the house of the Lord. **11** And they handed the money which was assessed over to those who did the work, who had the oversight of the house of the Lord; and they paid it out to the carpenters and the builders who worked on the house of the Lord."

Jehoash was very young when he became king but he did not let the older men influence him to do things that were not pleasing to God. Instead, he honored God even in a difficult situation.

Are you bold enough to do the right thing like Jehoash even when it is not popular?

Don't allow what people may think of you to influence the choices you make. Choose to please God even when you are standing alone. God will reward you for choosing to honor Him.

Psalm 147: 11
The Lord favors those who fear Him, Those who wait for His faithfulness.

PRACTICAL APPLICATIONS
House Rules!

FOR CHILDREN 4-6 YEARS OLD

Ask your parent(s) to help you write two of their house rules for you and help you to find a verse from this week's Torah reading that goes along with the house rules.

Write the verse and keep it on your wall or your desk as a reminder that when you honor your parents you honor God.

FOR CHILDREN 7-12 YEARS OLD

Make a list of your parent(s) house rules or school rules. Write a verse or two from this week's Torah reading that shares the same principle for the rules. Put your list on your wall or in a folder for school where you can see it every day as a reminder that when you honor your parents you honor God.

FOLLOW-UP FROM THE LAST TORAH PORTION

Ask who wants to share from last week's practical application Honoring God!

FOR CHILDREN 4-6 YEARS OLD

When you honor your parents you honor God.
Honor your parents this week in your obedience.

FOR CHILDREN 7-12 YEARS OLD

Each day this coming week, choose two of the Ten Words (Commandments) to learn and apply them as you go through your day.

QUESTIONS - TEACHERS ANSWER KEY

Dear Teachers,

The Q&A section for this week will be in a different format. Instead of giving the kids a list of questions to answer, we will present them with a scenario and have them decide what the right solution is based on the lesson from the Torah.

Scenario regarding stealing: Jeff's Candy Problem!

Molly gave Jeff a piece of candy, she told him not to tell anyone. She stole the candy from Sarah, but Jeff did not know she stole it.

David saw when she stole the candy and then gave it to Jeff, so he told Jeff what Molly did.

If Jeff decides to give the candy back to Sarah is that the right thing to do?

Should he give the candy back to Molly and tell her to return it to Sarah?

What is the best solution for Jeff's candy problem?

Things to consider when responding to kids' solutions to Jeff's problem.

Response: I think he should give it back to Molly, so Molly could give it back to Sarah. This way, he gives Molly a chance to make amends for her actions.

Response: *(Jeff's possible response if he hasn't eaten the candy)*
"Molly, I can't take this candy, as I know that it belongs to Sarah."

Response: Or was it enough that only David saw it? Shouldn't there be 2 witnesses?

I mean...we know the truth, but should Jeff just believe David on his word? Perhaps, he needs to go back to Molly and ask her.

Even though David said he saw her, Torah tells us we should have two or more witnesses.

Response: Is David guilty of Lashon Hara?
In this way, we encompass both commandments: how to make sure it's a true witness and properly make amends for the stolen candy.

Perhaps David needed to speak to Molly first. That he saw her stealing.

Molly should have a chance to tell her story

Response: We need to consider what was David's motive for telling Jeff he saw Molly stealing the candy.
Is David following the proper approach?

FINAL THOUGHTS

As we discussed in our lesson, God's rulings are not just a list of "dos" and "don'ts." God cares about His people. He cares about our relationship with Him and also our relationship with others. He is concerned with the way we value things. He wants us to understand that we should treat others, and their possessions, with the same love and respect we do for our own. We should honor him even when no one is watching us.

Our scenario focused on a few different rules; such as stealing, bearing witness or false witness, and speaking an evil report (Lashon Hara), all of which are wrong according to the Torah. It also hinted at the motive and the intentions of the heart.

We should at all times ask the Holy Spirit to help us make the right choices that please God. Although we will never know the motive or the intentions of someone's heart we can always check our intentions and motives when we do anything.

Proverbs 16:2

All the ways of a man are clean in his own sight, But the Lord weighs the motives.

Jeremiah 17:10

"I, the Lord, search the heart, I test the mind, Even to give to each man according to his ways, According to the results of his deeds.

QUESTIONS - CHILDREN'S COPY

Scenario regarding stealing: Jeff's Candy Problem!

Molly gave Jeff a piece of candy, she told him not to tell anyone. She stole the candy from Sarah, but Jeff did not know she stole it.

David saw when she stole the candy and then gave it to Jeff, so he told Jeff what Molly did.

If Jeff decides to give the candy back to Sarah is that the right thing to do?

Should he give the candy back to Molly and tell her to return it to Sarah?

What is the best solution for Jeff's candy problem?

CRAFTS SUPPLIES FOR TORAH PORTION MISHPATIM

SUPPLIES:
1. Colorful 12x12 Cardstock
2. Pen or Sharp Pencil for Writing
3. Markers, Pencils, Crayons
4. Gems, Stones, Sequins, Stickers

CRAFTS: TRUE REPORT

In this craft, children are going to get very creative! Since some verses in this portion talk about false reports, we are going to do a

TRUE REPORT!

Teachers, please take the names of all the kids and put them on small pieces of paper. Have each child pick a random name out of either a hat or a scarf, bucket, etc... (If they choose their own name, they should pick again. If there is an odd number of kids, then include the name of one of the teachers).

Then have the kids write a good and true report about a child that they picked! It should be about 7 different things. They could include facts: such as "Brielle has a baby sister", or an opinion, such as " Sophia is good at sports". If one child doesn't know that much about another child, they should do a little interview and ask questions about a child they had randomly chosen. They should all be life-speaking, uplifting statements.

After they have all their 7 points finalized, have the kids write them down on a piece of 12" by 12" colorful cardstock. Some kids might need help writing. They should include a child's name. Then they could draw a picture there. Decorate it with gems, sequins, and stickers. And at the end of the lesson, they will give it to the child they picked as a gift!

Here is an example of the True Report!:

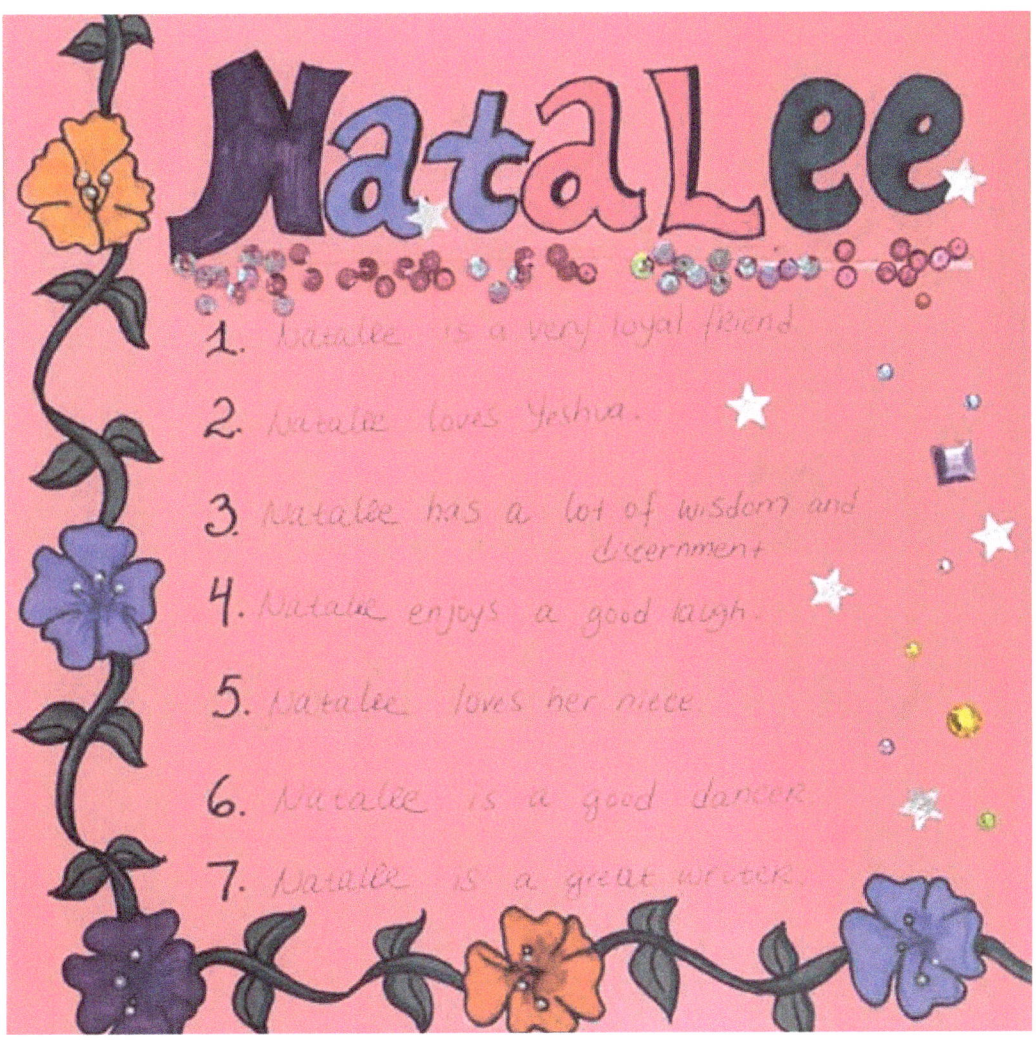

Terumah
"Contribution"

Torah Portion 19: Terumah

This week's Torah portion is called ***"Terumah"***, the Hebrew word translated as ***"contribution."*** It is found in the second verse of our Torah reading.

Exodus 25:2

Then the Lord spoke to Moses, saying, **2** "Tell the sons of Israel to raise a **contribution** for Me; from every man whose heart moves him you shall raise My contribution.

Scripture Readings:

Exodus 25:1-27:19, 1Kings 5:26-6:13, Mark 12:35-44, Psalm 26

The Theme of the Torah Portion:
According to the Pattern

Exodus 25:8-9 ESV

And let them make me a sanctuary, that I may dwell in their midst. **9** Exactly as I show you concerning the pattern of the tabernacle, and of all its furniture, so you shall make it.

Torah Portion Outline

- An Offering to the Lord, **Exodus 25:1-7**
- A Dwelling Place for God, **Exodus 25:8-9**
- The Ark of the Covenant, **Exodus 25:10-22**
- The Table of Showbread, **Exodus 25:23-30**
- The Menorah, **Exodus 25:31-40**
- The Tabernacle, **Exodus 26:1-13**
- Curtains, Hooks, Loops, and Cover, **Exodus 26:1-14**
- Boards and Sockets, **Exodus 26:15-30**
- The Veil, **Exodus 26:31-33**
- Arranging the Furniture, **Exodus 26:34-35**
- Screen for the Entrance, **Exodus 26:36-37**
- The Altar, **Exodus 27:1-8**
- The Courtyard, **Exodus 27:9-19**

LESSON SUMMARY

In our last Torah portion, Mishpatim Adonai wanted to speak with the entire congregation of Israel but they were afraid because of the loud thunder, smoke, and the sound of His voice. They thought for sure they would die if they continued to hear God's voice. They told Moses; to go and talk with God and then come tell them what He had said and they would listen. Moses received the rulings; Adonai's Commandments to teach the children of Israel.

In this week's Torah portion, God spoke to Moses saying to tell the children of Israel to bring Me an offering but they must give it willingly as a contribution from their heart. God requested thirteen different items: gold, silver, bronze, blue thread, purple thread, red thread, beautiful linen cloth, goat's hair, animal skin dyed red, onyx stones, acacia wood, oil for the light, and spices to make anointing oil, and sweet incense.

God also requested that the people should build him a tabernacle, a place for Him to dwell among them. He made it very clear that they were to build the tabernacle and all the furnishings for the tabernacle according to the pattern he showed Moses on the mountain. Each item the people brought as an offering was to be used to build the tabernacle and the different types of furniture to put in the tabernacle. God gave Moses every detail about the Tabernacle, its length, height, and length it was to be. He even told him what kind of materials to use, everything that goes in the tabernacle, and where they should be placed in the tabernacle.

The Tabernacle was designed with two rooms; the Most Holy Place, and the Inner Court. There also was an Outer courtyard. The tabernacle was made of boards overlaid with gold, and very decorative materials, held together with golden hooks and sockets. In it, they were instructed to make an ark and overlay it with gold. They also were to make its cover, called the Mercy Seat, with cherubim at one at each end, and overlay them with gold. In the ark were the two tablets with the Ten Words which Adonai gave to Moses on Mount Sinai. The ark was placed in the Most Holy Place in the Tabernacle. This is where God would meet the High Priest and speak with him. A table of Showbread and a golden menorah were also made and placed in the Inner court of the Tabernacle. They also made an altar for the offerings. It was made of bronze. The altar was placed at the entrance of the Tabernacle in the Outer court.

LESSON DISCUSSION

Exodus 25:1-9 Message Bible

God spoke to Moses: "**Tell the Israelites that they are to set aside offerings for me.** Receive the offerings from everyone who is willing to give. These are the offerings I want you to receive from them: gold, silver, bronze; blue, purple, and scarlet material; fine linen; goats' hair; tanned rams' skins; dolphin skins; acacia wood; lamp oil; spices for anointing oils and for fragrant incense; onyx stones and other stones for setting in the Ephod and the Breastpiece. **Let them construct a Sanctuary for me so that I can live among them. You are to construct it following the plans I've given you, the design for The Dwelling and the design for all its furnishings.**

God had three requests of the people in this Torah portion:
1. They were to bring Him an offering.
2. They were to build a sanctuary/tabernacle for Him to dwell among them.
3. They were to make the tabernacle and all the furnishings for the tabernacle according to the pattern He showed them.

God gave great details about how the Tabernacle and all its furnishings were to be made and where they should be placed within the Tabernacle.

If God gave such great details about the Tabernacle do you think He has great details about you?

Psalm 139:13-16 ESV — For you formed my inward parts; you knitted me together in my mother's womb. **14** I praise you, for I am fearfully and wonderfully made. Wonderful are your works; my soul knows it very well. **15** My frame was not hidden from you, when I was being made in secret, intricately woven in the depths of the earth. **16** Your eyes saw my unformed substance; in your book were written, every one of them, the days that were formed for me, when as yet there was none of them.

Matthew 10: 30 ESV
But even the hairs of your head are all numbered.

Did you know that God desires to dwell in you?
1 Corinthians 3:16 ESV
Do you not know that you are God's temple and that God's Spirit dwells in you?

Your body is a tabernacle, a place for God to dwell in by the Holy Spirit.

God wants us to offer our offerings to Him willingly.
1 Peter 2:5 ESV
You yourselves like living stones are being built up as a spiritual house, to be a holy priesthood, to offer spiritual sacrifices acceptable to God through Jesus Christ.

He desires for us to keep our tabernacle (our body) His temple according to His pattern.

Romans 12:1-2 Message Bible
So here's what I want you to do, God helping you: Take your everyday, ordinary life—your sleeping, eating, going-to-work, and walking-around life—and place it before God as an offering. Embracing what God does for you is the best thing you can do for him. Don't become so well-adjusted to your culture that you fit into it without even thinking. Instead, fix your attention on God. You'll be changed from the inside out. Readily recognize what he wants from you, and quickly respond to it. Unlike the culture around you, always dragging you down to its level of immaturity, God brings the best out of you, develops well-formed maturity in you.

TURNING POINT:

A PATTERN TO FOLLOW

Titus 2:7-8 — 7 ESV
Show yourself in all respects to be a model of good works, and in your teaching show integrity, dignity, **8** and sound speech that cannot be condemned, so that an opponent may be put to shame, having nothing evil to say about us.

God gave Moses a pattern (model) to follow to build the Tabernacle and all its furnishings. The commandments were a pattern for them and also for us to follow. God chose the children of Israel to be a pattern for other nations to follow, to learn, to serve, and to worship Him. God has a pattern for everything. Abraham was Israel's pattern to follow.

Yeshua is the pattern for us to follow.
John 15:9-11 ESV — As the Father has loved me, so have I loved you. Abide in my love. **10** If you keep my commandments, you will abide in my love, just as I have kept my Father's commandments and abide in his love. **11** These things I have spoken to you, that my joy may be in you, and that your joy may be full.

Are you a godly pattern (model) for your friends, family, and others to follow Yeshua? Everything you say and do is seen by someone even when you are not aware they are watching. Can they see your love for God the Father and Yeshua when you speak or in the way you treat others? Even the way you treat your personal items and what belongs to others is a representation of who you are and the model you are displaying.

Even when we think we have all the answers, we should always be a reflection of Yeshua, because all we have is given to us by Him.

When we model the pattern of Yeshua, we can turn to God for help and refuge when we are having a hard time. King David is also a great example of a pattern of someone who loved and followed God's commandments. He always prayed to God for help when he was in trouble. He also asked God to keep him on the right path.

Here is a prayer he prayed: "Declare me innocent, O Lord, for I have acted with integrity; I have trusted in the Lord without wavering. **2** Put me on trial, Lord, and cross-examine me. Test my motives and my heart. **3** For I am always aware of your unfailing love, and I have lived according to your truth. **4** I do not spend time with liars or go along with hypocrites. **5** I hate the gatherings of those who do evil, and I refuse to join in with the wicked. (Psalm 26:1-5)

We have great examples from the bible as patterns to follow. Your parents are also patterns to follow. Are you willing to be a pattern for some to follow?

PRACTICAL APPLICATIONS

My Parents, My Model — A Pattern to Follow.

FOR CHILDREN 4-6 YEARS OLD

This week try to do the things your parents do:

Examples: Pray when they pray. Read the Bible when they read, etc.

FOR CHILDREN 7-12 YEARS OLD

Choose one person who you think is a godly model (pattern) and ask if you can spend time talking with him/her about their routine for spending time with God. Use their routine as an example to follow and develop your own routine.

FOLLOW-UP FROM THE LAST TORAH PORTION

Ask who wants to share from last week's practical application

House Rules!

FOR CHILDREN 4-6 YEARS OLD

Ask your parent(s) to help you write two of their house rules for you and help you to find a verse from this week's Torah reading that goes along with the house rules.

Write the verse and keep it on your wall or your desk as a reminder that when you honor your parents you honor God.

FOR CHILDREN 7-12 YEARS OLD

Make a list of your parent(s) house rules or school rules. Write a verse or two from this week's Torah reading that shares the same principle for the rules. Put your list on your wall or folder for school where you can see it every day as a reminder that when you honor your parents you honor God.

QUESTIONS - TEACHERS ANSWER KEY

1. **List some of the items God asked the children of Israel to bring freely from their hearts to Him:** gold, silver, bronze, blue thread, purple thread, red thread, beautiful linen cloth, goat's hair, animal skin dyed red, onyx stones, acacia wood, oil for the light, spices to make anointing oil and sweet incense.

2. **After the children brought the offering to God, what did He ask them to do?**
Build Him a tabernacle for Him to dwell among them.

3. **What are the different pieces of furniture that were made for the Tabernacle?**
The Ark of Testimonies, Table of Showbread, the Mercy Seat, Menorah, Altar of Incense

4. **From where in the Tabernacle did God say He would speak?**
The Mercy Seat

5. **What was kept in the Ark of the Testimony?**
The two tables with the Ten Commandments

6. **Which two pieces of furniture were placed in the Holy Place?**
The Menorah and the Table of Showbread

7. **In which section of the Tabernacle was the Ark of the Testimony?** Most Holy Place

8. **How does God dwell among us today?**
Each answer will be different. Allow them to answer in their own words, then guide them. Through Yeshua, by the power of the Holy Spirit and Keeping His word.

9. **Which animal hair was used as a covering for the Tabernacle?**
Goat

10. The boards of the Tabernacle, the Ark of the Covenant, and the table of Showbread were overlaid with gold. **What was the altar overlaid with?** Bronze

QUESTIONS - CHILDREN'S COPY

1. List some of the items God asked the children of Israel to bring freely from their hearts to Him:

2. After the children brought the offering to God, what did He ask them to do?

3. What are the different pieces of furniture that were made to put in the Tabernacle?

4. From where in the Tabernacle did God say He would speak?

5. What was kept in the Ark of the Testimony?

6. Which two pieces of furniture were placed in the Holy Place?

7. In which section of the Tabernacle was the Ark of the Testimony?

8. How does God dwell among us today?

9. Which animal hair was used as a covering for the Tabernacle?

10. The boards of the Tabernacle, the Ark of the Covenant, and the table of Showbread were overlaid with gold. What was the altar overlaid with?

CRAFTS SUPPLIES FOR TORAH PORTION TERUMAH

SUPPLIES:
1. 12"x12" Cardstock of various colors
2. Gold Cardstock
3. Gold Wrapping Paper
4. Gold Paint
5. Brushes
6. Gold Embroidery Ribbon
7. Glue/Glue Stick
8. Red Cellophane Paper
9. Purple, Red, White, and Blue Pipe Cleaners
10. White or Light-colored Pencils

CRAFTS: TABERNACLE ITEMS:

1. The teachers will have one large tube of gold paint. Please give each student a drop of gold paint (as shown), and let them paint the stick gold. Allow it to dry.

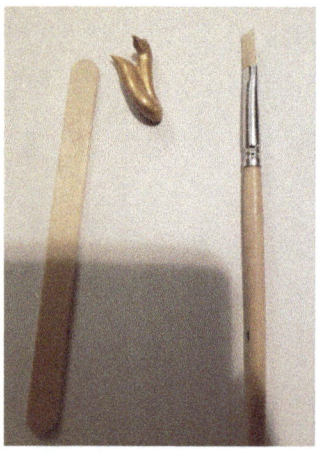 

2. While it's drying, the kids will work on the ark. On the gold body of the ark, put 2 strips of gold wrapping paper strips (on top and bottom as shown.)

3. On top, glue thick, gold embroidery ribbon. On the sides, glue thin embroidery ribbons. Leave some space not glued. You will understand why later.

4. Then glue the ark on the large construction paper in the bottom left corner.

5. Glue 2 cherubims on top of the ark, as shown.
6. Glue 2 wings of the cherubims as shown.
7. Take the gold-painted stick, and pull it through the thin ribbons as on the original artwork.

   The Ark of the Covenant part is done!

8. Children will receive 7 red pieces of cellophane to represent the menorah flames. These pieces will already be prepared for them.
9. Then each student will receive a pre-cut 7-branch lampstand. They will glue the red pieces of cellophane on the inside of each branch, as the original artwork. Double-sided tape is easier than glue.

10. Glue the menorah on the right side of the cardstock paper.
11. Finally, glue the colorful pipe cleaners at the bottom right corner.
12. Use a white pencil to show light coming out of the Ark.

    FINAL WORK

Tetzaveh

"You Are To Command"

Torah Portion 20: Tetzaveh

This week's Torah portion is called **Tetzaveh**, which means "**You are to command.**" It is found in the first verse of our Torah reading, Exodus 27:20.

Exodus 27:20 CJB

"Also ***you are to command*** Bnei-Yisrael *(children of Israel)*, that they are to bring to you pure olive oil beaten for the light, to cause a lamp to burn continually.

Scripture Readings:

Exodus 27:20-30:10, 1 Samuel 15:2-34, Mark 6:14-29, Psalm 65

The Theme of the Torah Portion:

For Beauty and Glory

Exodus 28: 1-2 ESV

"Then bring near to you Aaron your brother, and his sons with him, from among the people of Israel, to serve me as priests—Aaron and Aaron's sons, Nadab and Abihu, Eleazar and Ithamar. **2** And you shall make holy garments for Aaron your brother, for glory and for beauty.

Torah Portion Outline

- Oil for the Menorah, **Exodus 27:20-21**
- Garments for the Priests, **Exodus 28:1-4**
- The Ephod, **Exodus 28:5-14**
- The Breastplate, **Exodus 28:15-30**
- The Robe, **Exodus 28:31-36**
- The Turban (Head Covering), **Exodus 28:37-43**
- Aaron and His Sons are Consecrated, **Exodus 29:1-37**
- The Daily Offerings, **Exodus 29:38-46**
- The Golden Altar for Incense, **Exodus 30:1-10**

LESSON SUMMARY

In last week's Torah portion, God instructed Moses to take an offering from the children of Israel. He also requested that they should build a tabernacle for Him to dwell among them. God gave detailed instructions for building the Tabernacle and all the furniture that was to be placed in the Tabernacle. In this week's Torah portion, we learn about the garments that were to be made for the priests.

Aaron and his sons Nadab, Abihu, Eleazar, and Ithamar were chosen as Priests to minister to the Lord. The garments were holy garments for glory and beauty. "You shall speak to all the skillful, whom I have filled with a spirit of skill, that they make Aaron's garments to consecrate him for my priesthood. These are the garments that they shall make: a breastpiece, an ephod, a robe, a coat of checker work, a turban, and a sash. They shall make holy garments for Aaron your brother and his sons to serve me as priests" (Exodus 28:2-4). Aaron and his sons were consecrated for seven days for them to minister as priests before Adonai. Adonai also gave instructions for the daily offerings that were to be offered by the priest.

On the ephod, they were to put two stones, one on each shoulder. On the stones were the names of the twelve sons of Israel engraved in order of their birth. Six names were on one stone and six on the other stone. The ephod was also made with two golden chains which connected it to the breastpiece (breastplate). The breastplate was to be worn by the high priest (Aaron) to judge the people before Adonai. On the breastplate were also special stones. The stones represented the twelve sons of Israel. A robe was to be made of blue thread. Around the hem of the robe, there were small pomegranates made of blue, purple, and scarlet thread. In between each pomegranate, there was a golden bell. This was for Aaron the high priest to wear as he ministered in the holy place so the sound of the bell could be heard confirming he was not dead. A head cover was also a part of the priest's garments. It was called a turban. On the turban was a golden plate. On the plate was written, "Holiness To The Lord."

Aaron's sons' garments were different from his. Their robes were made of linen thread, a sash was made for them that went across their shoulders, and also a hat for their heads.

Adonai gave Moses instructions for the daily offerings to consecrate the Tabernacle where He would meet the children of Israel. Instructions were also given to make a golden altar that was placed before the ark of the covenant and the mercy seat. There Aaron would make atonement once a year for the people.

LESSON DISCUSSION

Similar to last week's Torah portion, Adonai gave Moses detailed instructions to follow for making the priests' garments. Last week we discussed the pattern God gave Moses to follow regarding the wilderness Tabernacle and its furniture, the commandments He gave to Moses on Mount Sinai, and that Adonai knew every detail about their lives. This week's lesson is about the garments for the priests who minister before Adonai. They were special garments. These garments were also a sign to all the people that Aaron and his sons were chosen by God to serve in His tabernacle and to minister to Him on behalf of the people.

Exodus 28: 29-30 ESV
So Aaron shall bear the names of the sons of Israel in the breastpiece of judgment on his heart, when he goes into the Holy Place, to bring them to regular remembrance before the Lord. **30** And in the breastpiece of judgment you shall put the Urim and the Thummim, and they shall be on Aaron's heart, when he goes in before the Lord. Thus Aaron shall bear the judgment of the people of Israel on his heart before the Lord regularly.

Did you know that as believers in Yeshua, we have special garments? We wear these garments so that others will know we belong to Him.

Ephesians 6:13-16
Therefore take up the whole armor of God, that you may be able to withstand in the evil day, and having done all, to stand firm. **14** Stand therefore, having fastened on the belt of truth, and having put on the breastplate of righteousness, **15** and, as shoes for your feet, having put on the readiness given by the gospel of peace. **16** In all circumstances take up the shield of faith, with which you can extinguish all the flaming darts of the evil one.

How do we put on Yeshua?

The garments of the priest were a sign to everyone that they were different; our actions and the words we speak should be a sign to others that we are different.

By the power of the Holy Spirit (Ruach HaKodesh), we are able to speak and do things differently to please God. The word of God calls it showing the fruit of the Spirit.

Galatians 5: 22-26

But the fruit of the Spirit is love, joy, peace, patience, kindness, goodness, faithfulness, **23** gentleness, self-control; against such things there is no law. **24** And those who belong to Christ Jesus have crucified the flesh with its passions and desires. **25** If we live by the Spirit, let us also keep in step with the Spirit. **26** Let us not become conceited, provoking one another, envying one another.

Are you wearing the right garment?

TURNING POINT:

Following Instructions

This week's Torah portion focuses on the garments that Aaron and his sons were to wear as priests in service to God. God gave Moses specific details for making each piece of the garments. Similarly to last week's Torah portion the details and the pattern are important to God. Even the offerings He requested from the children of Israel were specific. Their attitude was also important to Him; He only wanted the offerings they were willing to give Him.

God wanted the people to learn the importance of following instructions no matter how simple. He wanted them to choose to follow Him. Everything God presented to them, they had free will to obey or disobey. If they obeyed Him they would continue to live in His presence and receive His blessings and protection.

In our Haftorah reading from 1 Samuel chapter 15, God gave King Saul specific instructions, but he did not obey all that God told him. God wanted him to punish Amalek because he had attacked the Israelites when they came up from Egypt. He told King Saul to attack and destroy all Amalek had, but Saul did not obey God.

1 Samuel 15:10, 19-21

10 The word of the Lord came to Samuel: **19** Why then did you not obey the voice of the Lord? Why did you pounce on the spoil and do what was evil in the sight of the Lord?" **20** And Saul said to Samuel, "I have obeyed the voice of the Lord. I have gone on the mission on which the Lord sent me. I have brought Agag the king of Amalek, and I have devoted the Amalekites to destruction. **21** But the people took of the spoil, sheep and oxen, the best of the things devoted to destruction, to sacrifice to the Lord your God in Gilgal."

When we are not obedient to follow God's commandments (His instructions), He will not accept our offerings. God desires for us to obey Him but He will not force us to obey.

Are you willing to obey? Start by obeying your parents.

Ephesians 6:1-4 ESV

Children, obey your parents in the Lord, for this is right. **2** "Honor your father and mother" (this is the first commandment with a promise), **3** "that it may go well with you and that you may live long in the land." **4** Fathers, do not provoke your children to anger, but bring them up in the discipline and instruction of the Lord.

Colossians 3:20-24 ESV

But the fruit of the Spirit is love, joy, peace, patience, kindness, goodness, faithfulness, **23** gentleness, self-control; against such things there is no law. **24** And those who belong to Christ Jesus have crucified the flesh with its passions and desires. **25** If we live by the Spirit, let us also keep in step with the Spirit. **26** Let us not become conceited, provoking one another, envying one another.

PRACTICAL APPLICATIONS
The Armor of God.

FOR CHILDREN 4-6 YEARS OLD

Read Ephesians 6:13-20 with your parents and put on the armor of God every day.

FOR CHILDREN 7-12 YEARS OLD
Read Ephesians 6:13-20 each day and put on the armor of God.

FOLLOW-UP FROM THE LAST TORAH PORTION
Ask who wants to share from last week's practical application

PRACTICAL APPLICATIONS
My Parents, My Model — A Pattern to Follow:

FOR CHILDREN 4-6 YEARS OLD
This week try to do the things your parents do:
Examples: Pray when they pray. Read the Bible when they read, etc.

FOR CHILDREN 7-12 YEARS OLD
Choose one person who you think is a goldy model (pattern) and ask if you can spend time talking with him/her about their routine for spending time with God. Use their routine as an example to follow and develop your own routine.

QUESTIONS - TEACHERS ANSWER KEY

1. **What are the names of Aarons' sons?**
   Nadab, Ahibu, Eleazar, and Ithamar

2. **Which piece of garment had two stones on the shoulders?**
   Ephod

3. **What was written on the two stones?**
   Names of the 12 sons (tribes)

4. **How many stones were placed on the breastplate?**
   12 (twelve)

5. **What was the purpose of the (breastpiece) breastplate?**
   To judge the people before Adonai

6. **What was written on the golden plate of the priest's head covering?**
   Holiness To The Lord

7. **How can we put on Yeshua as a garment?**
   Wearing the Armor of God and showing the fruit of the Spirit

8. **What was the purpose of the priest's garments?**
   For beauty and glory

9. **Who gives us the power to show we belong to Yeshua?**
   Holy Spirit (Ruach HaKodesh)

10. **How can we serve others as an act of service to God?**
    Love our neighbors as we love ourselves. Treat each other with love and kindness

QUESTIONS - CHILDREN'S COPY

1. What are the names of Aarons' sons?

2. Which piece of garment had two stones on the shoulders?

3. What was written on the two stones?

4. How many stones were placed on the (breastpiece) breastplate?

5. What was the purpose of the (breastpiece) breastplate?

6. What was written on the golden plate of the priest's head covering?

7. How can we put on Yeshua as a garment?

8. What was the purpose of the priest's garments?

9. Who gives us the power to show we belong to Yeshua?

10. How can we serve others as an act of service to God?

CRAFTS SUPPLIES FOR TORAH PORTION TETZAVEH

SUPPLIES:
1. Gold Paper Crown for kids. Purchased on Amazon
2. Gems, Sequins, and Stickers
3. Glue

CRAFTS: Esther and Mordechai's Crowns

The children could wear their decorated crowns during the festive season of Purim.

Ki Tisa

"When You Take"

Torah Portion 21: Ki Tisa

This week's Torah portion is called **"Ki Tisa"**, the Hebrew word translated as **"when you take."** It is found in the second verse of our Torah reading.

Exodus 30:12 CJB
"**When you take** a census of the people of Isra'el and register them, each, upon registration, is to pay a ransom for his life to *Adonai*, to avoid any breakout of plague among them during the time of the census.

Scripture Readings:

Exodus 30:11-34:3, Ezekiel 36:16-38,
John 11:47-56, Psalm 75

The Theme of the Torah Portion:
Not Without Your Presence

Exodus 32:12-16 CJB

Moshe said to *Adonai*, "Look, you say to me, 'Make these people move on!' But you haven't let me know whom you will be sending with me. Nevertheless you have said, 'I know you by name,' and also, 'You have found favor in my sight.' **13** Now, please, if it is really the case that I have found favor in your sight, show me your ways; so that I will understand you and continue finding favor in your sight. Moreover, keep on seeing this nation as your people." **14** He answered, "Set your mind at rest — my presence will go with you, after all." **15** Moshe replied, "If your presence doesn't go with us, don't make us go on from here. **16** For how else is it to be known that I have found favor in your sight, I and your people, other than by your going with us? That is what distinguishes us, me and your people, from all the other peoples on earth."

Torah Portion Outline

- Money for a Ransom, **Exodus 30:11-16**
- The Brazen Altar (Lever), **Exodus 30:17-21**
- The Anointing Oil, **Exodus 30:22-33**
- Spices to Make The Incense, **Exodus 30:34-38**
- Wisdom to Build the Tabernacle, **Exodus 31:1-11**
- Remembering the Sabbath, **Exodus 31:12-18**
- The Sin of the Golden Calf, **Exodus 32:1-6**
- God's Anger Against the People, **Exodus 32:7-10**
- Moses Prayer & Smashing the Tablets, **Exodus 32:11-21**
- Aaron Tries to Explain the Golden Calf, **Exodus 32:22-29**
- Moses Prays for the People Again, **Exodus 32:30-35**
- God's Command to Leave Mount Sinai, **Exodus 33:1-6**
- Moses Meets with the Lord Outside the Camp, **Exodus 33:8-11**
- The Promise of God's Presence, **Exodus 33:12-23**
- Moses Makes New Tablets, **Exodus 34:1-9**
- The Covenant Renewed, **Exodus 33:10-28**
- Moses' Face Shines with God's Glory, **Exodus 33:29-35**

LESSON SUMMARY

For the past three weeks, we have been learning about the instructions that God spoke to Moses on Mount Sinai. In this week's Torah portion, we learn about the principles for counting the people, special spices to make the anointing oil to anoint the priest for service in the tabernacle, for making the incense to burn on the altar, and also for the two young boys chosen by Adonai to make everything He ordered Moses to make. Bezalel was chosen from the tribe of Judah. He was filled with the Spirit of God, with wisdom, understanding, and knowledge in all kinds of crafts, to make special designs of gold, silver, bronze, stone cutting, and wood carvings. Oholiab was from the tribe of Dan and was appointed to help.

While waiting for Moses to return from the mountain the people became weary and seemed hopeless without him. They did not understand why he had been gone for such a long time. They asked Aaron to make them a god to worship and follow. Aaron told them to bring their gold and jewelry, and with it, he fashioned a golden calf and presented it to them as their god. They offered offerings to the golden calf, they played music, and danced in worship as if it was the god who brought them out of Egypt.

Adonai told Moses what the people were doing. Adonai was angry at the people and wanted to kill them all, but Moses pleaded with Him not to destroy the people. He reasoned with God and said, if you destroy the people, other nations will hear of it and say, "It's because You were not able to bring them into the land You promised them." Adonai told Moses to go down to the people for they have turned away from following the path He had set for them, they are stiff-necked people. As Moses descended the mountain, Joshua, his assistant said to him, "It sounds like there is war in the camp." Moses responded that it was not the sound of victory or the cry of defeat. He said this knowing what they were doing. When they got close to the camp Moses saw the people dancing and worshiping the golden calf. He became enraged with anger and threw the two tablets from his hand at the bottom of the mountain. Entering the camp, Moses took the calf, melted it in the fire, ground it to powder, and scattered it on the water, then he gave the people the water to drink. As angry as Moses was with the people, the next day he went to pray and ask God to forgive them of their sin. God told him those who have sinned will be punished with a plague, but go and lead the people. Adonai reassured Moses that He would be with them and that He would send His angel before them. Moses was told to carve two tablets of stone out of the rock and to bring them to Adonai on the mountain so He could write His testimony on them again.

LESSON DISCUSSION

During the chaos with the golden calf, we discover something very special about Moses. Moses knew that nothing he had done since the day he saw the burning bush he accomplished on his own.

Exodus 33:12-16 CJB
Moshe said to *Adonai*, "Look, you say to me, 'Make these people move on!' But you haven't let me know whom you will be sending with me. Nevertheless you have said, 'I know you by name,' and also, 'You have found favor in my sight.' **13** Now, please, if it is really the case that I have found favor in your sight, **show me your ways**; so that **I will understand you** and **continue finding favor in your sight**. Moreover, keep on seeing this nation as your people." **14** He answered, "Set your mind at rest — my presence will go with you, after all." **15** Moshe replied, **"If your presence doesn't go with us, don't make us go on from here. 16 For how else is it to be known that I have found favor in your sight, I and your people, other than by your going with us? That is what distinguishes us, me and your people, from all the other peoples on earth."**

Moses had a personal relationship with Adonai. He spoke with Him as you would a friend.

Moses recognized in his relationship with God that he had favor but he desired more. He had a special relationship with God.

1. He wanted to know God's ways. (He was not satisfied with just hearing His voice.)
2. He wanted to understand God's ways to continue to find favor. He wanted to learn how to live for Adonai.
3. He wanted God's presence to go before him and the people because it is what tells the difference between them and the other nations of the earth. Without the presence of Adonai, they were just like everyone else.

Do you have a special relationship with God, our Heavenly Father?

Through Yeshua we can have a personal and special relationship with God; the Holy Spirit is the presence of God with us.

Ephesians 3:12 NLT
Because of Christ (Yeshua) and our faith in him, we can now come boldly and confidently into God's presence.

Without the Holy Spirit, we cannot understand the ways of God. John 14:26 MSG
The Friend, the Holy Spirit whom the Father will send at my request, will make everything plain to you. He will remind you of all the things I have told you.

Give children an opportunity to pray and invite Yeshua in their hearts.

TURNING POINT:

MY GOLDEN POOL - THE GOLDEN CALF

Can you imagine your parents going on vacation leaving you with your big brother or sister, and when they came back home there was a pool in the family room? How angry do you think they would be? This is what happened with Moses and the children of Israel in this Torah portion.

Well, Moses did not go on a vacation and the golden calf big brother Aaron carved was not a pool, but I think you get the picture.

Moses was still on Mount Sinai talking with God. The people thought for sure something must be wrong because he was not back yet. So instead of praying, or even asking Aaron to pray to God and seek answers, they told him to make them gods to go before them because they did not know what had happened to Moses.

Exodus 32:1-6 CJB

When the people saw that Moshe (Moses) was taking a long time to come down from the mountain, they gathered around Aharon and said to him, "Get busy; and make us gods to go ahead of us; because this Moshe, the man that brought us up from the land of Egypt — we don't know what has become of him." **2** Aharon said to them, "Have your wives, sons and daughters strip off their gold earrings; and bring them to me." **3** The people stripped off their gold earrings and brought them to Aharon. **4** He received what they gave him, melted it down, and made it into the shape of a calf. They said, "Isra'el! Here is your god, who brought you up from the land of Egypt!" **5** On seeing this, Aharon built an altar in front of it and proclaimed, "Tomorrow is to be a feast for *Adonai*." **6** Early the next morning they got up and offered burnt offerings and presented peace offerings. Afterwards, the people sat down to eat and drink; then they got up to indulge in revelry.

There are times when you don't understand why your parents or even God seems to take a long time to respond to your request(s) and you become impatient. In these moments learning to remain patient is the best thing to do. Sometimes you are tempted to do things on your own without adult supervision, and in doing so you make a big mess of everything.

Exodus 32:30-35 CJB

The next day Moshe said to the people, "You have committed a terrible sin. Now I will go up to *Adonai*; maybe I will be able to atone for your sin." **31** Moshe went back to *Adonai* and said, "Please! These people have committed a terrible sin: they have made themselves a god out of gold. **32** Now, if you will just forgive their sin! But if you won't, then, I beg you, blot me out of your book which you have written!" **33** *Adonai* answered Moshe, "Those who have sinned against me are the ones I will blot out of my book. **34** Now go and lead the people to the place I told you about; my angel will go ahead of you. Nevertheless, the time for punishment will come; and then I will punish them for their sin." **35** *Adonai* struck the people with a plague because they had made the calf, the one Aharon made.

If you have been disobedient like the children of Israel, you can still ask God to forgive you for your actions. Moses Prayed for the people and God answered him. God will forgive, just as your parents will forgive you for not obeying, but there will be punishment for your actions.

1 John 1:9 MSG

On the other hand, if we admit our sins—simply come clean about them—he won't let us down; he'll be true to himself. He'll forgive our sins and purge us of all wrongdoing.

PRACTICAL APPLICATIONS
KNOWING AND UNDERSTANDING GOD'S WAYS

FOR CHILDREN 4-6 YEARS OLD
Pray and ask God to teach you His ways when:
1. Talking with your parents
2. Talking with a friend
3. Sharing with others

FOR CHILDREN 7-12 YEARS OLD
Commit to asking God this week to show you His ways by asking Him in prayer.
1. Are you trying to know and understand God's ways?
   a. In your friendships
   b. In your conversations
   c. In your actions
2. Commit to knowing His ways through His word. Do you have a memory verse you want to learn this week?

FOLLOW-UP FROM THE LAST TORAH PORTION
Ask who wants to share from last week's practical application
The Armor of God

FOR CHILDREN 4-6 YEARS OLD

Read Ephesians 6:13-20 with your parents and put on the armor of God every day.

FOR CHILDREN 7-12 YEARS OLD
Read Ephesians 6:13-20 each day and put on the armor of God.

QUESTIONS - TEACHERS ANSWER KEY

1. Who were the two boys chosen by God to build all that God ordered Moses to build?
Bezalel and Oholiab

2. What was the name of Moses' assistant?
Joshua

3. Why did the people ask Aaron to make them a god?
They thought something happened to Moses

4. Where did Aaron get the gold from to make the idol god?
From the people

5. How did God describe the children of Israel, what kind of people?
Stiff-necked people

6. How was the testimony written on the two tablets?
By the finger of God

7. Which two tribes were Oholiab and Bezalel chosen?
Oholiab from the tribe of Dan, Bezalel from the tribe of Judah

8. What image did Aaron carve from gold?
Golden calf

9. What was the name of the mountain Moses met with God?
Mount Sinai

10. What did Moses tell God makes the difference between the Israelites and the other nations?
God presence

QUESTIONS - CHILDREN'S COPY

1. Who were the two boys chosen by God to build all that God ordered Moses to build?

2. What was the name of Moses' assistant?

3. Why did the people ask Aaron to make them a god?

4. Where did Aaron get the gold from to make the idol god?

5. How did God describe the children of Israel, what kind of people?

6. How was the testimony written on the two tablets?

7. Which two tribes were Oholiab and Bezalel chosen?

8. What image did Aaron carve from gold?

9. What was the name of the mountain Moses met with God?

10. What did Moses tell God makes the difference between the Israelites and the other nations?

CRAFTS SUPPLIES FOR TORAH PORTION KI TISA

SUPPLIES:
1. 12X12 Cardstock Paper
2. Tracing Paper
3. Cotton Balls
4. Plain Print Paper
5. Coloring Supplies: Markers, Pencils
6. Gold Cardstock Paper
7. Glue Sticks

CRAFTS: WE WORSHIP GOD ONLY!

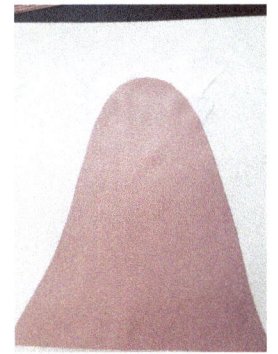

1. The kids will receive pieces of tracing paper cut-outs and glue them in the center top of the 12"x12" cardstock page. This represents the spirit.
2. Then they will receive cut-outs of Mount Sinai and glue them in the center as shown.
3. Then they will receive a pre-cut golden calf and place it at the bottom left of the page as shown.
4. In the next step, the kids will color in "angry Moses" cut-outs and place them at the bottom right of the page, as shown.

5. Then in the middle of Mount Sinai, they will put a statement "We worship only the God of Abraham, Isaac, and Jacob!"
6. On the right top corner, place a few pieces of cotton balls to represent clouds.
7. The last step: Kids will receive cut-outs of the "Mount Sinai" sign, drawn by Joel Calendrillo, an authentic Brooklyn artist.

   They will color it in and place the sign on the left side of the mountain.

FINAL WORK

VAYAKHEL & PEKUDEI

"And Assembled & Accounts of"

Torah Portions 22 & 23: Vayakhel & Pekudei

This week's Torah reading is from the Torah portions **Vayakhel** meaning **"He Assembled"** which is found in Exodus chapter 35:1 and **Pedudei** meaning **"Accounts"** which is found in Exodus 38:21.

Exodus 35:1 — Then Moses **assembled** all the congregation of *Bnei-Yisrael* and said to them, "These are the words which ADONAI has commanded you to do.

Exodus 38:21 — These are the **accounts of** the Tabernacle of the Testimony, as they were recorded according to the commandment of Moses, by the service of the Levites, under the hand of Ithamar son of Aaron the *kohen*.

Scripture Readings:
Vayekhel - Exodus 35:1-38:20, 1Kings 7:40-50, Psalm 61, Luke 22:1-13

Pekidei - Exodus 38:21-40:38, 1Kings 7:51-8:21, Psalm 45, Matthew 17:1-7

The Theme of the Torah Portion:

A Willing Heart!

Exodus 35:21-22
Then everyone came whose heart was stirred, and everyone whose spirit was willing, *and* they brought the LORD's offering for the work of the tabernacle of meeting, for all its service, and for the holy garments. **22** They came, both men and women, as many as had a willing heart, *and* brought earrings and nose rings, rings and necklaces, all jewelry of gold, that is, every man who *made* an offering of gold to the LORD.

Torah Portion Outline

- Offerings for the Tabernacle, **Exodus 35**
- More Than Enough, **Exodus 36**
- Construction of the Ark, Table of Shewbread, Menorah, and Altar, **Exodus 37**
- Altar of Sacrifice and Tabernacle of Testimony, **Exodus 38**
- Holy Garments for Aaron and His Sons, **Exodus 39**
- Setting Up the Tabernacle, Exodus 40: 1-33
- The Glory of God Fills the Tabernacle, **Exodus 40:34-48**

LESSON SUMMARY

In the past three Torah readings of Terumah, Tetzaveh, and Ki Tisa we have learned about the detailed instructions Adonai gave Moses for making the Tabernacle and all its furnishings. Last week we learned of Bezalel and Oholiab whom God chose to build and teach other wise-hearted people to complete the work for the Tabernacle. In this week's Torah reading, we see all the instructions God gave to Moses were carried out. The people brought their offerings, the materials for the building of the Tabernacle, all the furnishings, the priestly garments, the holy anointing oil for consecrating the Tabernacle and the priests, and the perfume for the incense.

Moses assembled the people and reminded them of Adonai's command to remember the Sabbath day. He also reminded them of the offerings to be brought to the Tabernacle. When the people brought the offering for the Tabernacle, Bazelal, and Oholiab told Moses to tell the people to stop because they had more than enough for all the work. So Bezalel, Oholiab, and the wise-hearted people constructed the Ark of Testimony, the poles to carry it, the Tent of Meeting and the three layers of covering, the Atonement cover, the curtain screen which separated the Holy Place from the Most Holy Place, the Table of Showbread, the Menorah and the pure olive oil, the Incense altar and its perfume, and the anointing oil. All that Adonai commanded was completed just as He had told Moses.

Moses commanded the Levites to take an account of the Tabernacle and the Testimony. Ithamar, Aaron's son was in charge of counting everything once the construction of the Tabernacle and all its furnishings were completed. They counted the gold, silver, and bronze that were brought to build the Tabernacle and all its furnishings. The garments for the priest were also made according to the specifications that Adonai gave Moses.

When all the works were complete they brought the tabernacle to Moses. Moses blessed the people when he saw that all the work was done according to all the words Adonai commanded. Adonai also gave Moses instructions to set up the Tabernacle on the first day of the first month (Nisan). The Tabernacle was set up in the second year after the children of Israel were brought out of Egypt on the first day of Nisan. Moses also washed Aaron and his sons with water as Adonai commanded him, in order to consecrate them as priests, and then he put the priestly garments on them. Once the Tabernacle was set up the cloud of Adonai covered the Tent of Meeting; His glory filled the Tabernacle, and Moses could enter it. Then the presence of Adonai rested on the Tabernacle by day as a cloud and by night as a pillar of fire.

Chazak! Chazak! Ve-nitchazek!

Be Strong! Be Strong! And May We Be Strengthened!

LESSON DISCUSSION

The Most Important Thing

We have learned of all the details and specific instructions God had given Moses to build the Tabernacle. It was time for Moses to give instructions to the Israelites to build it, but Moses did not start by telling them all the things they would need to bring to Adonai or the work that needed doing. Instead, he told them what seemed most important to Adonai.

Moses Assembled the congregation of Israel and said, these are the things that Adonai says you must do. "On six days work is to be done, but the seventh day is to be a holy day for you, a Shabbat of complete rest in honor of Adonai. Whoever does any work on it is to be put to death. You are not to kindle a fire in any of your homes on Shabbat."

Moses gathered the people to tell them about the offerings and all the things they needed for Bezalel and Oholiab to begin building the Tabernacle.

Moses first tells the people about Adonai's commandment to remember this Sabbath day, and then he tells them about the offerings and everything else. Moses reminded the people about Adonai's command to keep the Shabbat because it is a holy day unto Adonai.

It is a reminder for us that no matter what work we desire to do for Adonai, obeying His command to honor the Sabbath is the first work we must do.

Exodus 34:4-9 CJB

Moshe said to the whole community of the people of Isra'el, "Here is what Adonai has ordered: 'Take up a collection for Adonai from among yourselves — anyone whose heart makes him willing is to bring the offering for Adonai: gold, silver and bronze;" "blue, purple and scarlet yarn; fine linen, goat's hair, tanned ram skins and fine leather; acacia-wood; oil for the light, spices for the anointing oil and for the fragrant incense; onyx stones and stones to be set, for the ritual vest and the breastplate."

Moses' second instruction to the people was directed to all who were willing to bring an offering to Adonai. The people brought all that was requested. They brought more than what was needed to build the Tabernacle.

"The Israelites, all the men, and women, whose heart moved them to bring material for all the work, which the Lord had commanded through Moses to be done, brought a voluntary offering to the Lord." Exodus 35:29 NASB2020

When we give to Adonai, we should give willingly with a cheerful heart.

2 Corinthians 9:7 CEB

Everyone should give whatever they have decided in their heart. They shouldn't give with hesitation or because of pressure. God loves a cheerful giver.

Remember, honoring the Sabbath is the first work we do unto Adonai because it is His holy day, and when we give or whatever work we desire to do for Him we must do it with a willing heart.

TURNING POINT:

My Silver Lining: Count Me in

In last week's Torah portion Ki Tisa, we learned that Moses was ordered to take a count of all those twenty and older, and they were to bring half a shekel as a ransom for their lives so that a plague would not break out on them.

Seems pretty strange right?
That's what I thought. In the middle of God giving Moses instructions for building the Tabernacle, he tells him to count the people 20 years of age and older. What does counting have to do with building a tabernacle? In this week's Torah portion in Exodus 38, we read where Moses was given instructions to take account of all the materials that were used to build the Tabernacle; all fabrics and linen, the gold, silver, and bronze.

Here is the record of the half-shekel that was given by those who were counted in the Torah portion Ki Tisa.

"The silver obtained from those of the community who were counted in the census was 100 talents and 1,775 shekels, according to the sanctuary shekel— one beka per person, that is, half a shekel, according to the sanctuary shekel, from everyone who had crossed over to those counted, twenty years old or more, a total of 603,550 men. The 100 talents of silver were used to cast the bases for the sanctuary and for the curtain—100 bases from the 100 talents, one talent for each base. They used the 1,775 shekels to make the hooks for the posts, to overlay the tops of the posts, and to make their bands." **Exodus 38:25-28 NIV**

All the silver shekel collected from the count was used for the frame of the tabernacle. The tabernacle was standing on a silver lining.

Things that seem strange and out of the ordinary to us are very important to God. You are very important to Him, even if you don't feel as if you are important to anyone. You are a silver lining, you count!

PRACTICAL APPLICATIONS

Honor the Shabbat.

FOR CHILDREN 4-6 YEARS OLD

Help your mom prepare for Shabbat this week.

FOR CHILDREN 7-12 YEARS OLD

Help your mom prepare for Shabbat this week.

FOLLOW-UP FROM THE LAST TORAH PORTION

Ask who wants to share from last week's practical application.

KNOWING AND UNDERSTANDING GOD'S WAYS

FOR CHILDREN 4-6 YEARS OLD

Pray and ask God to teach you His ways when:
1. Talking with your parents
2. Talking with a friend
3. Sharing with others

FOR CHILDREN 7-12 YEARS OLD

Commit to asking God this week to show you His ways by asking Him in prayer.
1. Are you trying to know and understand God's ways?
    a. In your friendships
    b. In your conversations
    c. In your actions
2. Commit to knowing His ways through His word. Do you have a memory verse you want to learn this week?

QUESTIONS - TEACHERS ANSWER KEY

1. How many days should we work?

6 days

2. Which day of the week is the Sabbath day?

The 7th day

3. Why is it important to honor the Sabbath?

It is God's holy day.

4. Complete the verse "...God loves a _____ giver!"

(cheerful)

5. When was the Tabernacle first set up?

In the second year on the first day of the first month after leaving Egypt (Nisan 1)

6. How many years after the children of Israel left Egypt was the Tabernacle built?

Two (2) years or second year

7. Why couldn't Moses enter the Tabernacle when it was set up?

The glory of God filled the Tabernacle

8. How did God lead the people?

Cloud by day and fire by night

9. What was Moses' command to do to Aaron and his sons before they wore the priestly garments?

Wash them with water

10. What other event happened in the first month of Nisan?

Passover

QUESTIONS - CHILDREN'S COPY

1. How many days should we work?

2. Which day of the week is the Sabbath day?

3. Why is it important to honor the Sabbath?

4. Complete the verse "...God loves a _____ giver!"

5. When was the Tabernacle first set up?

6. How many years after the children of Israel left Egypt was the Tabernacle built?

7. Why couldn't Moses enter the Tabernacle when it was set up?

8. How did God lead the people?

9. What was Moses' command to do to Aaron and his sons before they wore the priestly garments?

10. What other event happened in the first month of Nisan?

CRAFTS SUPPLIES FOR TORAH PORTION VAYAKHEL & PEKUDEI

SUPPLIES:
1. Various Colors of 12x12 Cardstock
2. Silver Cardstock
3. Plain White Cardstock
4. Gold Tissue Paper
5. Red Cellophane Paper
6. White Fabric
7. Print Paper
8. Red or Orange Pencils
9. Glue Sticks
10. Double Stick Tape

CRAFTS: EREV SHABBAT!

Children will do the craft that has to do with the traditions of Shabbat evening. After they finish with the craft, if time allows, make the girls in the class practice how to recite the prayers by pretending that they are lighting up the candles, praying over them, and the bread/wine.

1. First, children will receive a set with two silver candle holders made from silver cardstock. They will glue them in the middle of 12"x12" cardstock paper.
2. They will glue little gold ovals at the top (as shown) to represent the gold inside.
3. In the next step, they will glue candles for each holder and draw flames with red or orange pencils.
4. On the right side, they will glue silver challah plates.

5. They will color the challah and glue it on top of the plate.
6. With the double stick tape, they will attach the white fabric to represent the challah cover. Please ONLY attach the top edge of the fabric so the rest of it is loose, and you can lift it and see the challah under.

7. On the left-hand side, glue the wine cup cut-outs. On top of it, glue red cellophane that represents the wine.
8. The last step will be gluing pre-cut Hebrew/English prayers, as shown.

FINAL WORK

About the Authors

Natalee Henry began her personal faith journey in 1996 with a burning desire to live an extraordinary life for the Lord. Since then, the Lord has kindled a passion within her for sharing and teaching the Word of God.

In 2016, God answered Natalee's prayer for spiritual growth when she was introduced to studying, learning, and implementing the Torah way of life as a believer in Yeshua. Natalee is a Torah-observant believer learning to honor God's Appointed Times and serving within her local congregation to all ages.

Natalee is an author, motivational speaker, and founder of the Season Destiny Ministry designed to "***empower youths to make the right decisions in life.***" Natalee is a graduate of International Seminary Bible College, and authored ***Seasons of Life-Taking Man Back To God***, 2005; ***Embracing Destiny***, 2010; ***Overcome to Fulfill Your Purpose: Become Successfully You***, and ***Successfully You, Leadership Training Workbook*** 2018, and her most recent, ***Making Transition Through Crisis: A Rebuilding Guide for Young Professionals***, 2021.

Natalee has a passion for young people and seeks to share with them that they do not have to 'settle' for being less than God created them to be; nor do they need to succumb to today's culture, lies, and worldliness.

**Yevgeniya Calendrillo** was born and raised in Ukraine to a secular Jewish family. Growing up, Yevgeniya yearned for a relationship with God for many years. By the age of 24, she was married and living in the United States. Yevgeniya and her husband are entrepreneurs and business partners selling their artwork and also are heavily focused on nutrition and health. Yevgeniya and her husband have one son, whom she homeschooled for 3 1/2 years.

Yevgeniya was invited to a Messianic congregation in Brooklyn where she accepted Yeshua as her Savior; and opened the Bible for the very first time. Yevgeniya has been a Messianic believer for over 20 years.

Yevgniya has a Bachelor's degree in Fashion Design from the Fashion Institute of Technology, New York. Yevgeniya has many years of experience in the New York fashion industry. Yevgniya is an artist who is gifted in watercolor painting. She recently discovered her talent for children's crafts and utilizes her knowledge, and experience in arts and design, as tools for investing in children for the Kingdom of God. Yevgeniya is currently serving as Children's Ministry Leader and a children's Torah teacher at Save The Nations.

Yevgeniya has a passion to follow God, to be obedient to His Torah instructions, to seek Him diligently, and to walk in her calling to teach Torah and Hebrew lessons to children.

About the Book

Shemot (Book 2: Exodus) is a part of the Torah Curriculum for children, covering the first five books of the Bible. This curriculum is based on the weekly Torah Portions so they may learn Torah in a simple and practical way.

The Lessons are structured so our children will learn from the Torah Portions and see the connection with Yeshua (Jesus), and the work of the Holy Spirit. Our aim is not just to give information but to teach Torah principles and demonstrate how to use them in their lives.

Each lesson is designed as a guide for teaching the Torah Portions to children ages 4 to 12 years. This curriculum is filled with creative crafts designed by Yevgeniya and insightful lessons written by Natalee.

Visit our website at www.torah4children.net to learn more about other books from our curriculum and our ministry.

www.ingramcontent.com/pod-product-compliance
Lightning Source LLC
Chambersburg PA
CBHW081331230426
43667CB00018B/2899